Published in Great Britain by
L.R. Price Publications Ltd, 2021
27 Old Gloucester Street,
London, WC1N 3AX
www.lrpricepublications.com

Cover artwork by L.R. Price Publications Ltd
Copyright © 2021

Used under exclusive and unlimited licence by
L.R. Price Publications Ltd.
Peter McDonald Copyright © 2021

The right of The Author to be identified as author of this work has been asserted in accordance with sections 77 and 78 of the Copyright, Designs and Patents Act, 1988.

Peter McDonald

MEMOIRS OF EARLY WORKING LIFE

Peter McDonald

Peter McDonald

Dedication

To my wife Christine and my daughters Karen and Julie who stood fast through thick and thin and Freddie Elliot who was always there to give welcome advice.

Peter McDonald

Preface

I first started writing this viewpoint, of what work was really like in the 1960s and 1970s, in 1981 – when things were changing in such a way that it was my opinion the consequences would be suffered for many decades.

This view of working life in the sixties and seventies is far removed from journals of the so-called "permissive society", and that of swallowing purple hearts and being beatniks. All we wanted was a job which gave some security, and a wage one could live on. Most of us earnt just enough to get by and have a drink at the weekend. If we had any money in the bank it was not very much, and if we lost our jobs would probably only keep us going for a week or two – if we were lucky.

It was at a time when we were apparently all on strike, lazy and abusing the welfare state. Yet, unemployment levels were at their lowest in history.

The simple truth was that if you wanted some security, and a wage sufficient to pay the bills, you needed to join a union and fight for it. It seems to me that nothing has changed.

Peter McDonald

Contents

1. *Plenty of Work, Not a Lot of Cash*
2. *Civilization of Sorts*
3. *Heart Attack*
4. *What's Cooking?*
5. *Piecework Comes to The Zoo*
6. *Overtime Kills You*
7. *The Unwelcome and Unplanned Strike Begins*
8. *The First Casualty of the Strike: The Milkman*
9. *They Are All Scabs Now*
10. *Nice Countryside Trip to Kidderminster*
11. *Not Just a Battle, But a War*
12. *Resolution in Sight*
13. *A Burning Issue*
14. *Siege of Kelly's Office*
15. *Peace Time*
16. *Outbreak of War*
17. *Battle Lines Being Drawn*
18. *Battle Lost*
19. *Directed into the World of Education*
20. *The Struggle Continues*

1

Plenty of Work, Not a Lot of Cash

By June 1962, at the age of fifteen, I'd had enough of school and left.

I started my first job working on a farm, which was situated on the slopes of the Lickey Hills, on the outskirts of Birmingham. As a child, I always wanted to tread the fields of Earth, but never could. I could now walk the land at will – or so I thought.

I started work in the early hours each morning. At six o'clock, we started loading up the milk floats with crates of milk. It was a dairy farm, comprising friendly Jersey herds. Huins Farm, as it was known, was run by Mr. Huins himself, and his son Stan.

Old man Huins was a skinny bloke, of medium height. He would follow me around, and if I was unfortunate enough to make the slightest mess, I would receive a lecture on how to not do the job in a way which created another. Ironically, this would come in handy in later years, when trying to justify man-hours for trade union members.

His son didn't have a good word for anyone, and an awful habit of spitting every few minutes. He would greet you by looking at his watch and saying, "Morning, come on, we gotta get a move on," then spit wherever he was standing. The milk was delivered in the morning and the cows milked and fed in the afternoon. Chickens also had to be fed and eggs collected – all under the watchful eye of spitting Stan.

I managed to stick the job for eight months, right through the horrible winter of 1962/63. But, farmers… what a breed! I seriously wondered if Mr. Huins counted the blades of grass! They definitely counted each egg individually, each bottle of milk – even the nuts and bolts. And they were experts at counting the seconds it took me to drink a cup of tea! The meaning of "tea break" was just that – exactly as long as the tea lasted. If it was too hot to drink, tough; Stan would say, "Come on we have work to do," spitting to emphasize his displeasure.

This was my first encounter with the concept of "performance-related" pay; to receive payment I had to "perform", by feeding the cows, watering them, giving them hay and mucking out. Of course, I also had to collect the eggs and still have time to milk the cows. I really did *perform* in order to carry out such tasks, with a bale of hay on one shoulder, a bale of straw on the other, one hand carrying a bucket of water and the other a bucket of cow cake. This performance was the only way I could earn my pay.

A good friend of mine at the time, John – who was my age, with a rather loud Brummie voice – became a fellow employee. I recall that I was struggling to perform one afternoon, and had just managed to sneak around the side of the barn for a breather, when I bumped into John, who was with Stan.

"You bloody fool!" Stan suddenly shouted. "You don't give them all that together; you will make the bloody cows ill!" He had an affinity with the word "bloody".

"It is the only way I can get the work done on time," I replied.

"You are bloody lazy and bloody useless!" Stan said. He turned to John and said: "*Never* do what he is doing. Do the job properly, not like that bloody fool!"

With that, I dropped the bales, pulled out one of the pitchforks and held it to his throat. "You sod!" I said, menacingly. He didn't respond; he looked scared.

Then, thinking that I had performed remarkably well, I put the pitchfork down and went on my way. I couldn't help thinking to myself how similar this situation was to Kennedy threatening Castro at the time, over the missile crisis. There was Stan, with his wealth, power and authority, and there stood I, with my pitchfork.

I left his employment shortly afterward, but never forgot that you can never do enough for a gaffer! That is, a (spit) bloody (spit) gaffer!

2

Civilization of Sorts

From farming, I entered the more "civilized" environment of the Gun Quarter. Here, we had set breaks for meals and indeed a cup of tea. I became an apprentice barrel-filer, with famous gunmaker W.W. Greener's. The building was well over a hundred and fifty years old, and most of the gunmakers never seemed to retire; they just carried on indefinitely. The building I worked in was really an operational museum. It consisted of small working shops, usually with no more than four or five working in each one. Each person had their own vice and cloak hook. For heating, there were two stoves, one at each end of the workshop, fuelled by coke.

The job of the apprentice was foremost to keep the stoves alight, by fetching and carrying coke. We also had to fetch anything needed from the shops and, of course, sweep and generally keep the place clean. However, a key part of apprenticeship was to be ridiculed. My first few months were spent trying to avoid being "Christened", but it was inevitable, and accomplished in style (having your testicles painted with Indian Ink!).

Colin was the gaffer – the man who taught me and John the trade. John was better known as "Speedy", because he was slow at picking things up. Speedy was muscle-conscious but of medium build, pigeon-chested and wore thick-rimmed glasses.

The eldest of the apprentices was Rodney, who was about to come out of his time. Although Colin was the gaffer in the shop, he had no authority over Rodney. Rodney was a free spirit, and so trendy that he would go on about The Beatles before they had ever made a hit record. Every Monday morning, for the first hour Rodney would describe in detail what he had been up to over the weekend. More importantly at the time, he would also give us the entire lowdown on Christine Keeler. It was just as interesting to watch him as to listen to him, mainly because the first hour on a Monday was like playing charades; it made the mind boggle with intrigue, observing his version of what had gone on with Christine Keeler.

Colin was in his early thirties, and obviously had troubles with his anus. There was not a hole in his body where he did not put his fingers. We all mimicked him behind his back, mainly because he came over as a person who couldn't take a joke, and would probably not know what a joke was, anyway. Additionally, Colin always let it be known that he was our gaffer, and we should never forget it. He had a nasty habit of coming over to one's bench, removing whatever might have been in the vice and saying: "Christ, this is rubbish!" He would then throw it over his shoulder, onto the floor.

"Pick it up and bring it over to my bench," he would then say; "watch me and learn" – he would then set to work on whatever we had been doing. Rodney would be jesting throughout and making the situation worse, inasmuch as we could not dare to laugh, through fear of what Colin might do to us.

At the time of my "Christening", Colin was more than helpful to the engravers from the next-door shop who performed the task – his card was thus marked by me.

Another annoying habit, out of which Colin seemed to get a great deal of delight, was that if he knew you were going out that night and wanted to get away early, he would do his best to see that you did not. His favourite trick was to screw your workbag to the bench – as if not satisfied with that, he would then file the screws, so it became extremely difficult to free the bag. I once had a go at him for this, which ended with me receiving a salt and vinegar hair shampoo! It was most certainly here that I first learnt

Memoirs of early working life

how to take a joke – because the more I complained, the more fellow workers seemed to enjoy what was happening to me.

1. At the age of fifteen, working at W. W. Greener's.

Speedy developed a new meaning for the word "sooner". When we needed to use the toilet, we had to go down three flights of stairs and across the yard. The stairs were the original ones, wooden and rickety. Often, some clown would grease the banisters, and the first person out would slip and tumble down the flight of stairs; we would hear an almighty noise and someone shouting: "You bastards!" So, Speedy suggested that, instead of risking the stairs, we could go upstairs to the empty shop and use the old fountain in the corner as a toilet – sooner up there than all the way across the yard. Hence, the term "going for a sooner". Colin was never told of this, and thus never knew what a "sooner" was.

It was time to get our own back on Colin. One day, Rodney, Speedy and myself got together, and Rodney said: "It's his anniversary next Wednesday; he'll be wanting to get away early."

"Right," I said, "I'll teach him a lesson. I'll nail his shoes to the stool."

Speedy added, with enthusiasm: "I'll keep the bugger in the muffle room, by burning a barrel while you do the business."

The next Wednesday, at 3.30 p.m., smoke came pouring from the muffle room.

Colin shouted: "What's that prize prat Speedy up to now?

He'll burn the place down." And, off he marched into the muffle room, arms swinging and chest out.

That's when I nailed his shoes to the stool, and Rodney nailed the lid of his desk down. Unlike the rest of us, Colin changed both his shirt and shoes before starting work, hence he needed access to his desk for his shirt, tie and going-home shoes. Who could also forget that his desk had been handed down to him by his grandfather – as he told us on numerous occasions?

Ten past four arrived: time to pack up. Colin walked over to his desk and attempted to lift the lid. Then he squealed once, went red in the face and began shouting and swearing: "Which clever bastard's done this?!" I thought, *Well, if Rodney's a clever bastard, then what will that make me, when he goes to put on his shoes?*

After splitting the lid of his desk, Colin gained access to his shirt and tie – and I watched with bated breath; what would he do next? He bent down as he normally did, grabbed his shoes… and the stool came with them.

"Christ almighty!" he screamed.

I thought: *Yes, Christ is indeed almighty, but Christ didn't do it.*

"The no-good bastard!" he screamed, now in a right state. So, while Rodney was "clever", I was just "no good"?

And, with Colin still cursing and banging on, I left to catch my bus home – well, I didn't want to be late, did I?

Next morning, Colin said to me: "I know you wouldn't have done such a thing – my shoes ruined, along with my grandfather's desk. And, on top of everything, I wanted to get away early to celebrate my anniversary."

"What bastard could have done such a thing?" I replied.

"You never know what people are capable of. My dad said to trust no one, especially at work," added Speedy.

So confident we were now, we decided to really hit Colin, once and for all – using Speedy's "sooner". Every Friday afternoon, we would go through the ritual of Colin trying to teach us how to braze – people from downstairs and next door would come and watch the spectacle. The teaching usually consisted of myself and Speedy being ridiculed by Colin. So, Rodney suggested: "While he is with one of you, brazing in the corner, why don't the other one go for a "sooner", right above the brazier? Just make sure Colin is the one doing the brazing!" Great idea, we all agreed. However, Rodney was poor at keeping a secret, and told his mate David of the plot. David still saw himself as a Teddy Boy – a hard knock.

So, it's Friday afternoon and, as usual, Colin says: "Come on, Mac, you're going to learn to braze, whether you like it or not." So, off I went brazing. Then, in walks David from downstairs; he isn't going to miss a thing.

"God blimey," he offers, "good job you're in charge, Colin; he can't braze to save his life."

"I know," replied Colin. "It's no good; give it here, I'll have to show you again how it's done. Look at yourself: you're a right prat, Mac."

Having seen enough, Speedy pipes up: "I'm going for a 'sooner'."

I gently moved back away from the burner, giving the impression I was impressed by Colin's skill. A few seconds later, a drizzle of water started to fall on the brazing bricks.

"Bloody leaking roof," said Rodney. David's face started to beam at the thought of what was coming next.

Then, a trickle splashed on Colin's head. He ignored it; "When the temperature is right, you've got to keep going, no matter what." Within a couple of minutes, water was running down Colin's face, all over the brazing area.

"It's time that bloody maintenance crew repaired that roof proper!" protested Rodney.

"What a stink! Worse than boiling piss!" stated Colin, as he grappled with his work.

By this time I was too frightened to laugh or speak. But "clever bastard" Rodney was still going on about the leak. "It ain't good enough that water's stale! They don't give a piss in this place," he shouted, earnestly. David was buckled up with laugher.

The door of the shop then opened and Speedy walked in. "God, it's pissing down!" he shouted.

"It's not too bad now," replied Colin. Well, we certainly had Speedy to thank for that laugh.

Brazing completed, Colin returned to his bench, covered in a mixture of sweat and urine. By finishing time that day, there wasn't an employee there who didn't know what had happened. People from next door and downstairs were coming into the shop to look at Colin, and he was not aware of the reason; he thought they were coming in to ridicule Speedy and I for not being able to braze. After the umpteenth person had looked him over, he shouted: "I'm pissing—" a tremor of fear went through my body, as I wondered where this was going, "—fed up with everyone looking at us as though it were a zoo. Pissing me off!"

3

Heart Attack

In 1966, Harold Wilson had put an arms embargo on South Africa, and South Africa was a major customer of Greener's. Orders were lost and work became less busy. Month after month I found myself playing "split the kipper" with Speedy: two opponents stand a few feet apart, facing each other, and one throws a knife to stick in the wooden floor, a reasonable distance from one of the opponent's feet – if the knife doesn't stick, it doesn't count. The opponent then has to move his foot to where the knife is, without moving the other foot, pick up the knife and take his turn. And so on, back and forth. To win, you have to be the first to force your opponent into a position where they either fall over or can't make the required move.

Eventually, I was released from my apprenticeship and began work at B.S.A. Guns in Redditch. The company was huge compared with Greener's, employing in excess of two thousand people. The skills that I learnt at Greener's allowed me easily to champion any gun I was asked to work on. However, the place was very formal, with a foreman, superintendent and manager: the foreman to watch over the workers, a superintendent to watch over the foreman watching over the workers, and a manager to watch over the superintendent watching over the foreman who was watching over the workers.

When I told my father I was going to work at B.S.A., the first thing he said was: "Get yourself in a union, straight away. The benefit of a big company is that there is usually a good union." I thought immediately of the car industry, where unions were respected and would strike at a drop of a hat. I had never been on strike, and began to look at it as an adventure, fighting the well-to-do.

I started work in what was called a "cage". It was isolated from the rest of the shop (working area) by thick wire mesh, and had three benches inside it. Outside of the cage were machines, and the odd office to accommodate a foreman. Our foreman Paddy Kelly had his office just outside the cage, next door to the superintendent's office.

Paddy Kelly was of medium height and slim build. He had a fascination for walking around and visiting people as they worked; what he lacked between his ears he made up for by using his feet.

If you objected to his frequent visits and crass overtures, he would increase his visits. He was like a milkman doing a round, forever trying to increase customers by making more deliveries; he even wore the white coat with blue lapels and cuffs. Paddy didn't just walk; he sprinted. One Wednesday, when I was bored to tears, I followed him on his visits. It was like a grand tour; he went from one shop to another at a sprint, never stopping until he arrived at the area he was responsible for. Then, he would harass whoever he could, for work.

Next door to my cage were the assembly lines, where Terry, an old friend of mine from the Gun Quarter, worked; he assembled air rifles, as did at least another ten people. Terry was a skinny bloke of medium height, and wore glasses. Although he was in his early thirties, he acted like he was in his early twenties. Every Friday dinner I would join him and three others he worked with, and go for a drink. One of those I got pally with was Colin, a friendly bloke, who warned me that Terry had a bad reputation where he lived, and to watch out for him – whatever that meant. The other was Lionel, who was nineteen (one year younger than me), and the only one who actually lived in Redditch. Then there was Len who, like Colin and Terry, was in his late thirties. Len called a spade a spade, and gave the impression that if you didn't like what he had to say, he would easily follow it up physically.

I worked in the cage on one of the company's more expensive weapons, known as the Martini. It was mainly used for target shooting, and hence had some status. My main job was to fit the body – or breechblock, as it is probably better known – to the barrel. Having worked at Greener's, I had little difficulty in doing this, although fitting the body was extremely difficult, which of course made me feel quite important.

I shared the cage with two others: Jack, who was in his late fifties, and Bill, who was the same age. Bill was a Londoner, and always went on about London. He had no previous experience of gun-making, and had only been on the job three months before I started. Bill was a machinist, whose job had become redundant with the introduction of new machinery. Rather than be made redundant himself, he accepted an offer of working on the bench in the cage. He was a friendly bloke, who never had a bad word to say about anybody; a bit overweight, but nothing out of the ordinary for a man his age. Jack, on the other hand, was slim, of medium height and nimble, with previous gun-making experience.

However hard you worked, it just was never good enough for Kelly. If he could get away with pushing anyone – especially the older ones – he would do so with glee; Kelly revelled in harassing people. Although I found little difficulty with the job, Jack occasionally experienced problems, and poor old Bill did quite often. Bill was frightened of Kelly's visits, and would often – due to the harassment he received from Kelly – scrap the odd breechblock. These bodies were worth quite a few quid, so Bill would hide any he had scrapped in his bench drawer, then, when the opportunity arose, throw them in the scrap bin. Jack, on the other hand, was a sly bloke, and you would never know if he scrapped anything; he kept everything close to his chest.

Kelly would often visit Jack, but I had little idea what they talked about. The only thing I knew for sure that they discussed was overtime. Apparently, before I joined them, Jack worked regular Saturdays and Sunday mornings. Naturally, he saw me as the reason for him losing his overtime. Jack had a nasty habit, toward the end of any conversation with Kelly, to put his hand over his mouth and talk from the side of his mouth, at the same time waving his hand. He reminded us all of Whistling Jack Smith – hence we called him "Whistling Side-mouth Jack Smith". Covering his mouth and waving his hand gave the impression that he was saying something untoward to Kelly, who always responded by nodding and winking.

I recall watching Jack once, who seemed to be having a

problem fitting a body. Then, after a while, he walked round to Bill's bench and put the body he had been working on in Bill's bench drawer (Bill was not there at the time). Occasionally, when Bill was having difficulties, he would ask me to do a body for him, to save him getting into trouble with Kelly for not doing enough. Kelly would make up to twenty-four visits a day to the cage. I felt quite guilty at that moment, after all the bad things I had said about Jack to the lads next door, when we went for a drink.

Many times, on a Friday afternoon we would sing "On Mother Kelly's Doorstep". If we had enough to drink we would change the words and sing: *"He's got a hole in his sock, a hole in his shoe, a hole in his ass where his brain shows through."* Because the four of us would sing it at Kelly as we returned from the local pub, he would never say a word.

Kelly would frequently come into the cage and mutter the same diatribe. "For Christ's sake, Bill! You have got to do more than that," he would say.

"I'm getting there, Paddy; don't worry," Bill would reply. Kelly would then go and speak to Whistling Side-mouth Jack. This would really get our backs up, because none of us knew what they were saying.

On his way out, Kelly would often say to me: "How many

have you done?"

"Not enough," I would reply, knowing you can never do enough for a gaffer.

At times, when Kelly left the cage Bill would stop work, lean on the bench and just look down at the floor. He was petrified of losing his job.

I had just had a good week. The weather was nice, I had just witnessed Jack doing some work for Bill, and since Wednesday Kelly had not made that many visits to the cage. What's more, I was to get engaged that Saturday, so I was looking forward to my Friday afternoon drink with the lads from next door.

We had just sat down in the pub, to enjoy a drink, when Colin suddenly said, in anger: "What's that bastard Kelly doing to Bill?"

"What do you mean?" I replied.

"His wife's been on to me; Kelly is worrying the poor bloke to death, the toe rag."

"Well, Kelly does keep on at him, but I thought things were improving; Bill doesn't seem too bad at the moment," I replied. I had obviously been too full of myself to notice that things were worse than ever.

With the alcohol flowing and tempers rising, we all agreed to stop Kelly before he killed Bill off. "From now on, if Kelly comes pushing any of us, we'll tell him to piss off," said Colin. "Agreed?" We all agreed. I couldn't wait to tell Kelly to piss off, knowing I had the lads behind me (how far behind me, I didn't realize).

The following Monday, at about 9.50 a.m., just before our tea break, I noticed Kelly having one of those conversations with Whistling Side-mouth Jack, when Bill was out of the shop. This time, I distinctly heard the words "bloody scrapped bodies" coming from Side-mouth. With that, they both walked over to Bill's bench, opened his drawer and took out a breechblock. "Bleeding crap!" said Kelly, as he stormed off.

Poor old Bill didn't return until well after the break at about eleven o'clock. Kelly had had him in the office with the manager and superintendent, one watching the other giving Bill a final written warning. Bill was now in a right state, his face puffed up as red as a beetroot. His eyes were full of water and he was incapable of filing because his hands would not stop shaking. *How can anybody be treated like this?* I thought. Bill had fought in the war, so that people like me could enjoy a life free of fascism – yet here he was, not a trench in sight and not a weapon to defend himself, the victory he secured over twenty years ago slowly being killed off. At least in the war he would have been able to shoot dead the fascist – and receive a medal for doing so!

I went straight to the union steward, who did her best to rally support. Then I went to the lads next door, hoping that Bill would receive their support.

"Bill should have told Kelly to piss off!" said Terry.

"That's right," shouted Colin.

"Stupid bugger got himself in that position," said Len.

At least Lionel said: "We ought to do something. Poor old bloke."

"What are you going to do? Go on strike?" laughed Terry.

I soon came to realize, the more I discussed it with them, just how great a distance they were behind me. I went back to the stewardess, who had done her best but couldn't muster much support, mainly because Bill wasn't in the union. What's more, the overwhelming majority weren't, either. *Christ, I thought, I wish this was the car industry.* From that minute onward, because of what I'd learnt that day, I never believed for one moment the reports of bad practices in relation to union activities in the car industry – or any other industry.

The continued harassment of Bill by Kelly continued. I couldn't fathom why Jack had set Bill up, by dumping what I now know to have been a scrap body in his bench drawer. What had

Bill done to Side-mouth to deserve such a thing? I did my best to dirty Jack's name, but most people didn't want to know. They didn't want reminding that they had done nothing to help Bill in a deliberate setup.

It was now Monday again, a week to the day since Bill had received his final warning for poor work, and he had not come into work. At ten o'clock, Colin came into the cage.

"Mac, I have just been speaking to Bill's son."

"Oh, yeah?"

"He is dead, Mac. He died of a heart attack over the weekend," Colin said.

"You're not serious! He can't be dead," I said, not really believing the words. "What caused his heart attack?" I then said, forcefully.

"The job. His son said the job was getting him down; he did nothing but worry about losing it," Colin answered, sheepishly.

Colin then left the cage and I was left with my thoughts, still trying to get to grips with why people like Jack and Kelly would treat a fellow human being the way they had. I was devastated, shocked… I had witnessed first-hand how a person in authority could legally kill someone. The foreman had all the power and no social responsibility for his actions. *How can a country which brags about democracy allow one of its citizens to be killed like this?* I thought. We had enjoyed one of the largest peace movements in Europe, demonstrated against the U.S. war in Vietnam and took direct action against the white tyrants of South Africa. How could we let Bill die? How could it happen? Why did it happen? And what could I do about it?

Why was Kelly still foreman? To me, he was a murderer, and his accomplices were the manager and the superintendent watching Kelly doing it.

The answer became obvious: because we were not all in a union.

There were movements throughout the country, all with their own liberal ideas, but the true defender of the working people was the Trade Union Movement. The union didn't just move on holidays and high days; it moved every day. Only the Trade Union Movement challenges a so-called democracy which allows people to have unaccountable power over others' daily life. Foremen, superintendents and managers have immense power over the lives and time of their employees, yet they are never required to stand for election and thus canvas support. Yet, for the majority of the working class, they have more power than politicians – the politicians they see every so many years; gaffers they see every working day of their life.

By Wednesday, most of us were working as normal – certainly Side-mouth Jack and Kelly were. That afternoon, Kelly came into the shop and said to me: "Can you give us an extra two today, Mac?" He wanted to make up for the loss caused by Bill's death.

"You'll have what I do," I replied.

"Now, look here, you'll do the extra two whether you like it or not!" said Kelly.

"Bleeding clear off!" I replied.

At that, his forefinger started to prod at my shoulder, as he rained abuse on me. Bill immediately flashed through my mind; I punched him and squared up. Within ten seconds he had retreated and went on one of his many walks.

I never heard anything more about the incident, although it was the talk of the shop. The last time anyone had talked so much about an incident was when I went to the stores to get some files and stumbled on a couple having it away.

Bill's funeral was to be held the following Monday. Side-mouth Jack had been asked by Kelly to work over on the Saturday and Sunday, prior to the funeral. I learnt that Jack would never join a union, to fight for better wages and conditions, and therefore eliminate the *need* to work over by receiving a living wage;

instead, he would collude with an unelected person in authority to hound someone into an early grave, just to gain overtime. *Not all tyrants are in South Africa,* I thought to myself; *greedy, crass fools will kill you in this country, for little more than extra work, more hours and more pay.*

I left shortly afterward, a more experienced person, who appreciated the importance of being in a union. Had we been organized, any harassment of Bill would have been harassment of us all, and all of us would have struck against Kelly.

4

What's Cooking?

It was still 1967, and I was trying my hand at being a cook in a hospital kitchen. Nothing too demanding, and the money wasn't good, but I was intending to get married the following June.

We worked days and late evenings. The cook on evenings would cook whatever the "Evening Book" dictated, and one should never deviate from those instructions. It was a Tuesday evening and I was on lates (evenings). I entered the kitchen and went straight to the Evening Book, to see what was on. There wasn't much to prepare: pork chops, chipolatas, bacon, liver, chips and peas for the matron on duty. This was prepared to the best of my ability. When the meal was ready, I asked the matron's secretary to deliver the meal to the matron. At first, the secretary refused to take the dinner to her.

"The matron will go barmy," the secretary said; "she'll never eat this in a month of Sundays!"

A Month of Sundays, I thought, *what a great title for a Beatles song – or even better, a protest song by Bob Dylan.* I wouldn't have minded a month of Sundays: at least I would get some time off.

"Take it," I said to her, as tears became apparent in her eyes; "you shouldn't be scared of anybody." I showed her the Evening Book, which clearly stated what I had prepared. "Look, that is what I have been told to prepare, and that is what the matron is going to receive." Realizing that the secretary was frightened of the matron just made me even more determined that the matron was going to receive the meal. She might frighten the secretary, but she wouldn't frighten me. Eventually, the secretary went on her way with the meal.

Within a few minutes the secretary returned, with the meal untouched. "She won't have this. She's gone mad. You must ring her immediately," the secretary said, in a most disturbed way.

"I have no intention of ringing her, or anyone else, for that matter," I replied, cockily. As the secretary left the kitchen again, the phone started to ring.

I found this quite annoying, as I was about to start my break. I picked up the phone and said: "Kitchen."

The matron was on the other end and she was fuming. "What do you think you are doing sending me this dinner? How dare you? I am Jewish," she said, very angrily.

I replied: "I didn't think—"

"You have no right to think. How dare you think?" she said.

Again, I thought straight away of a title for another protest song: "You have no right to think. How dare you think?" *Bob Dylan could do something with this. He could link it to the Vietnam War.*

To be told off is one thing, but to be told you've no right to think is quite another. Assuming that she must be a fascist, I just put the phone down, got my coat and went home. As far as I was concerned, I had left the hospital's employment.

The following day, the kitchen's superintendent rang my home. Fortunately, I was not in and my father took the call. The superintendent was full of apologies and what have you. Someone had played a prank, putting the wrong meal in the Evening Book. No doubt the matron had made some enemies, and one or two were getting their own back. I didn't really care; by then I'd had enough of the place anyway, and was pleased to have an excuse to leave.

5

Piecework Comes to the Zoo

That Thursday, I had an unexpected phone call from my old gun-making friend Terry. "Kelly wants you back in the cage. The Guns are moving back up to Birmingham." The Guns had originally been situated in Birmingham, alongside the parent company B.S.A. Motor Bikes. It had only moved to Redditch some five years earlier, to take advantage of the cheap rates of pay and government subsidies.

I was out of work and the prospect of the dole was not attractive to someone who was shortly to get married. "Okay, what do I do?" I asked.

"Your actual interview will be in Birmingham, at the Small Heath site, where you will work until The Guns move up from Redditch in six weeks' time. And Kelly won't be interviewing you; a Mr Day will be."

I was to go for my interview at 9.30 a.m. on Friday. I arrived in my best suit, though the interview centred mainly on money.

"How much are you receiving at the moment?" asked Mr. Day, the personnel manager.

Naturally, I didn't inform him that I had just left my employment and that I was on ten pounds a week. "Twelve pounds a week at the moment," I replied, trying my luck.

"Good, we will pay you the same for the first four weeks," he replied.

"Okay, when can I start?" I asked.

"As soon as you can," he replied.

"Well, I don't believe my employer will object to me leaving straight away. I'll start Monday, if that's alright," I said, tongue in cheek.

"Yes, fine. You will be working in the woodshop, sanding until The Guns arrive, in about six weeks' time. Then, you will move into the cage under Mr. Kelly. Until then, your foreman is a Mr. Matthews," Mr. Day replied.

I wasn't too worried about Kelly's crass overtures. We would be in Birmingham, and I was sure there would be a union, which wouldn't stand for him harassing people.

The woodshop had been run down over the last few years, losing most of its work to Italy. It had been reduced in size to a mere fifth of what it originally was, to make way for the gun assembly and machinery, with a skeleton crew of just ten. There had only been one significant investment, in a German machine known as a Gigor. This machine had the technology to do ten people's work, thus producing stocks in a much-reduced area, which became attractive to management, leading to fewer stocks being imported from Italy. I was put to work with the main sander, known as Sid.

He was in his early forties, and was the youngest in the shop. Sid didn't just sweat; he sweated bucketfuls at the mere thought of work, which created a terrible odour. He also didn't just smoke; he chain-smoked, which meant he was out of the shop a great deal of the time, having a break. Sid had only recently returned to the woodshop after spending two years working on the motorbike side. He had originally been on the sanders for the previous ten years, before the rundown.

The sanding machines dated back to well before the First World War; they were estimated to be well over eighty years old. There were eight sanding machines, all converted to electricity from overhead belts. Each machine shaped a particular part of the stock, and the process carried out was that of a production line.

The main business in Birmingham was the production of motorbikes. The Bikes employed some 3,000 people, compared to the 350 employed on The Guns. We were situated across the road from The Bikes, which gave us a separate identity.

Sid was a big bloke, over six foot in height and 14 stone in weight. When he put pressure on a stock, the sander instantly removed the wood in a great cloud of dust.

Wagger was a skinny little bloke, very friendly and never without a smile. He seemed to work everywhere: on sanding, the bench, the machines and in the spray shop. Wagger was in his late fifties, and would always nod and smile, in response to anything you might have said. An inoffensive sort of a bloke, who always had difficulty breathing and was a perpetual yellowy colour. He was very helpful, and would never get into a deep conversation or argument with anyone.

Situated at the back of the sander was Tom, aged at least sixty-six. He had spent most of his working life with The Guns and was the most experienced bench hand. Tom dressed like someone from the late 1920s: flat cap, muffler and stud shirt. He had worked through the Second World War, right up to the present day, and had managed to keep working continually for forty years. He was of slim build and his shoulders were permanently bent over, as though he was working on a bench. Tom had acquired his own personal bench, tools, cupboards and a couple of lockers. Even though he had managed to keep his job all those years, he was no creep – just competent at his job. Tom had no difficulty socializing, while at the same time keeping a fair distance from you. Tom had been on fire duty in the Second World War, on the night B.S.A. received a direct hit; he would give an insight of what it was really like at the time the bombs were raining down.

Peter McDonald

2. Working on the sanding machines. Sid is to my left, working the sanding drum.

Also working on the bench was Alfie. He was deaf and had difficulty talking. A pattern maker by trade, Alfie was of medium height and weight, at sixty-one years of age; a loveable bloke, who would go out of his way to help you. Because of his deafness, when talking to you he would wave his hands about, jesting, his body bent backwards and his eyes glowing. He worked mainly on the bench, hand sanding the company's most prestigious butts. However, because of his tendency to enjoy a conversation, he was known as the gossip of the shop, and thus little attention was paid to what he said.

Near Alfie worked Arthur, who was also deaf, though spoke more clearly than Alf. He was of medium height and slightly overweight, in his late fifties. Unlike Alf, Arthur was a bit of a goer; he told people in no uncertain manner what he thought of them, and would not think twice of following it up with his fists. His toughness disappeared when called into the office, though, where he would only use sign language and act very sheepishly, giving the impression that he was a saint. Arthur had been involved in a nasty accident some years earlier, when he was struck down by a stacker truck; the injuries he sustained left him with "loco movement" (staggering from one side to another when he walked). He was a single bloke who lived with his sister and brother in-law.

Quite often, Arthur would help me on the sanding when Wagger went missing. I soon found out that Wagger visited the toilet at least six times a day to be sick – he was obviously ill, but chose to keep his illness to himself. Unlike Arthur, Wagger was not in a union.

Across the shop from the sanders was where the main machines were. The man responsible for operating the machines was David. There were fourteen machines in all, and David knew the procedure in which to operate the stocks. David was an Irishman, with a stomach that protruded like a balloon. He always wore a flat cap, frequently moving it and pushing his hand over his hair, which was greased flat over his head. Whenever he talked, his hand would take the shape of a fist, with a thumb up, as though he was pointing behind him. His clothes were old, dirty and worn; there was never a piece on his body which didn't have a hole in. He was in his mid-fifties, smiled a lot and was easy enough to get on with. Being the main machinist, David knew the ropes. He never walked from one machine to another; he shuffled. His looks and style were reminiscent of the 1940s.

David was a strong Catholic – a single man who took delight in the fact that he had a three-bedroom house to himself. He would often say, "I don't need money like you youngsters; look at this," then produce a wad of notes from his pocket. David was always the first to arrive at work in the morning – at least an hour before anyone else. He would settle down to a cup of tea and read the paper, as a preparation before starting work. Over the years, he had managed to accumulate two lockers, a table and a couple of cupboards. This enabled him to create a nice little niche, where he couldn't be observed easily, allowing him a crafty smoke. David's first act of work each morning was to turn on the extractor fan – it was so noisy, it acted as a bull to call the rest of us to work.

Most of us got on alright with David, except for Alfie, whom David just never had a good word for, referring to him as "that stupid, gossiping dummy". A contradiction, I thought, if there ever was one.

Also, David would never have his holidays at the same time as everyone else; he would religiously take his annual holiday over three weeks before everyone else, who kept to the main holidays. The only reason I could think of for him to do this was to be able to work the main holidays and gain overtime payment for it. David worked overtime regularly, saying: "I don't need this overtime, but how else are you going to get enough work?" As the main machinist, he supplied the bench hands and the sanders with work, then, of course, the sanders kept the spray shop going, which in turn sent the finished stocks to their destination.

David always spent his breaks with Henry, who was known as "H". Henry was the shop's sprayer; his shop was next door to the sanders, and he could be seen twice an hour walking past the sanders, on his way to the toilet for a smoke. Although both David and Henry smoked, David could stop coughing, whereas Henry couldn't. Henry would put this down to the fact that he had to get up three times a night for a smoke, and while awake smoked two fags an hour.

What he didn't tell you, but others in the shop would, was that in previous years he and Wagger would clean the ducting out at weekends and holidays, to get the overtime. The ducting, with the help of the extractor fan, took the dust to the large bins outside the shop for disposal; it was just large enough for a person to crawl through. The poor extraction would lead to a build-up of dust in the ducting, which would eventually lead to no extraction at all. So, they would both volunteer to clean out the ducting, and obviously this could not be done in work time, while the fan was running; it had to be done outside of working hours. They would clean the ducting by crawling through and using a hand scraper, to remove the clogged dust from the wall of the ducting. They never wore masks or harnesses – no wonder they were both suffering; it also explained why they both looked as though they were in their seventies. When I asked Wagger if this were true, he proudly answered: "Of course we did; we'd spend all weekend scraping and crawling. We didn't need masks in them days; we were men."

Farther up the shop, toward the bandsaw (for cutting shapes in wood) worked Jack, aged 62 years. He was of slim build, quite tall, with fair, receding hair. Jack was the shop's spindler – a friendly bloke, who always acknowledged you by putting his thumb up. He would brag that he started work at the end of the Great Strike (1926) and still had all of his fingers, which was unusual for a spindler. Jack ticked over relatively steadily, and took little nonsense from the gaffers. He acted as the unofficial shop steward for his little area, being a member of the Wood Machinists' Union.

Behind Jack, on the bandsaw worked Eddy, also aged 61 years and of slight build, but a lot smaller than Jack. He wore glasses and gave the impression of being a nasty bit of stuff – but, in fact, the opposite was the case: he would help anyone, and openly admitted to being a union member. Eddy had no time for gaffers and saw them as creeps; he constantly moaned about the gaffers and was a joy to listen to. He had lost his wife and children in a bombing raid in the war, and devoted most of his spare time to the St. John's Ambulance Brigade, where he was a respected superintendent. At meetings, Eddy would be short and sharp, and never failed to use his favourite expression: "Bulls' bollocks!" (emphasizing *bollocks*).

The person responsible for moving all the part-finished work around the shop, from one operator to another, was Aziz the labourer, who was in his late forties. One of his most important jobs was to see that he returned from the local cafe with the right order! A man of slim build, he liked to drink coffee and tea mixed. Although his command of English was not brilliant, he had little difficulty doing what was required. Doing a job kept him in work; every time we did any work we made a mess, and Aziz would clean it up. Thus, in doing a job we created another job, which gave someone a job and helped the economy along.

All of those old-timers had learnt to get by just ticking over; just doing enough: making the job look as difficult as possible to do, and indeed to understand. Any shortcuts and tricks of the trade were kept close to their chests. As Eddy would repeatedly say: "Bulls' bollocks, keep them (management) as ignorant as possible, else they'll stick a broom up your arse and expect you to sweep the floor as you work." Well, as time went by, there was evidence to support Eddy's theory. We were treated like donkeys, with a carrot and a stick; whistled to like a dog. Eddy often said: "Give us a broom and I'll put it on the end of my plod; you're working me like a horse, so I might as well look like one."

My first couple of days in the woodshop were quite pleasant. The sweet smell of wood and shaping stocks on the sanding machines was a novelty. However, by the following week my nose was blocked up and I couldn't smell a thing. I just kept saying to myself: "There's only six weeks to go." Sid did his best to show me how to do the job, and Wagger would often help me out, although with his frequent visits to the toilet, he wasn't that much of a help.

I found it extremely difficult to find out just how much everybody was earning. I recall trying to find out from Sid. "How much are you on? I'm on twelve pounds a week," I said.

"Well, that ain't bad, but I am on more," he replied.

"How much more?" I asked.

"That's my business, not yours," he replied. "It's enough."

I felt very uncomfortable at this and thought I would ask Alfie, as he was such a friendly bloke. I walked over. "How much you on a week, Alfie?" I asked.

"Can't tell you," he answered; "the gaffer would go mad."

So, eventually I walked up the shop to Eddy and asked: "How much do you earn a week?"

"You don't tell anyone here how much you are on," he said: "if they think you're on more than they are, they will cut you up."

"Come on. We should all know what we're on and act as one. We shouldn't be hiding our wage packets from anyone," I insisted.

"No doubt you're right, but with this crowd they'll never tell you the truth; they would rather hang you than work with you. Bulls' bollocks, they would dig their grandmothers up for a shilling, given half a chance," he said, as he slammed a blank piece of wood on the bandsaw table. "They have stabbed me in the back in the past, and I'm just covering it now," he went on to say, looking over his shoulder at David.

After a couple of weeks, the gaffer started to talk seriously about increasing production on the sanding. The foreman Mr. Matthews never seemed quite with it; he was in his late fifties and seemed to be on another planet – a good guise for a gaffer. Sid was in his office a couple of times a day with Matthews, discussing how production could be increased. Of course, I knew the answer: I was to work harder. Not the gaffer; me. Production would increase, because Matthews had said those inspiring words: "It's in all our interests to work harder and increase production.

Furthermore, it's just as hard for me as it is for you."

Rather than making the gaffer's job – or my job – any harder, I felt it my duty *not* to improve production. Matthews already suffered with arthritis and, being in his late fifties, work might have killed him. So, after four weeks the production never increased, so another sander joined us, from over in the bikes department.

John was known as "Ginger", because of the colour of his hair, and was the same age as me. We had a lot in common, particularly when it came to putting pressure on Sid, to go along with any of our ideas for the sanding. As the work decreased at The Bikes – because of the onslaught of poor investment coupled with the Japanese economic invasion – the surplus labour was being transferred to The Guns, as it increased its production. Hence, my consideration for the health of the gaffer had created a job for someone else, who might have had only the prospect of the dole to look forward to. And, the more of us who made a mess, the more secure became the labourer's position. Indeed, extra help was now required for the labourer.

Six weeks passed and The Guns had not arrived. No one really knew when they might be coming, just that they were. Realizing I might be in this dust-ridden place for some time,

Ginger and myself decided we would improve conditions by calling the unions in. We managed to call in the convenor from the motorbikes: a big six-footer, with the weight to go along with his height. He was known as Big Aus, and on the day he walked into the shop, things changed. Immediately we were given masks, to protect us from the dust – though too late for Wagger, whose daily visits to the toilet were becoming more frequent; his skin was becoming darker and his lips had turned black. Yet, he continued to keep smiling and nodding, as he always had done. The rumour was that he was suffering from cancer.

Big Aus managed to get everyone in the shop in the union. Although he was a big bloke, he came over very meek and mild; his build afforded him that privilege, which made him very approachable. We were now organized and democratically elected our representative – not like the gaffers, who imposed their representative on us. We could now challenge the gaffers; we had protection from the evil of authoritarianism. We had our R.S.P.C.A., in the form of a union – for Eddy was right: we were treated like animals. Donkeys with a stick and carrot; horses, the way we worked; and sheep, the way we were often led to slaughter and kept in a zoo, for the gaffer and his mates to come and visit.

By the ninth week I had a day off, preparing for my wedding.

Big Aus called a meeting of the shop and I was elected shop steward (or, more appropriately, "R.S.P.C.A. Officer"). As new shop steward, Big Aus warned me that, from meetings he'd had with the works manager – a Mr. Hole – the honeymoon of day work was over: the gaffers were going to introduce piecework (payment by results), to increase production. *Christ,* I thought, *if working as we were was a honeymoon, then I'm not looking forward to getting married!*

Ten weeks had now passed, and The Guns still had yet to move in. I was beginning to settle down, and started to get a great deal of satisfaction settling disputes and generally improving conditions. I started to learn just how powerful people are when they stick together, and was now starting to appreciate the meaning of the saying *"Divided we fall, united we stand."* It was at this time that Matthews called me into the office, to tell me we all had to move to piecework in the shop – and he had decided that the sanders should be the first. The three of us on the sanders agreed we would work as a pool (putting all our work together and equally sharing out the earnings). And, of course, myself and Ginger knew what conditions Sid had worked under in the past, and we weren't going to have him negotiating poor wages and conditions; Ginger and myself had no intention of crawling through ducting to make up our wages.

Monday morning at ten o'clock people came to visit the sanders in smart suits. They turned out to be the "time study" people. I wondered how you could have the time to study time. They stood over us, clipboard in hand and a clock which had a hundred seconds to the minute! They had managed to increase the working time by forty per cent – a marvellous achievement, considering they hadn't lifted a finger! They stood over us for an hour, recording everything we did. We were truly animals in a zoo, and these were the lion-tamers. These well-groomed people would decide how hard we had been working, how hard we should work and what price we would receive for the job; if we didn't work hard, then we wouldn't receive any food, because our wages would be low. The stick we were being tamed by was the price being offered for the job. We soon sussed them out, taking longer to do the job, while at the same time putting more effort in.

I had now worked in the woodshop for twelve weeks, The Guns hadn't moved in and all the shop – bar sanders – had agreed prices. Everyone had invented ways of doing the job longer, even inventing fictitious operations to get the best price. However, whatever price was being offered, the sanders were refusing; with three people, it's harder to get a common agreement, which meant that the price had to be agreeable to all three – hence, it had to be good. Mr. Hole (works manager) decided to see us, along with Big Aus, in his office, over our refusal to accept the prices being offered.

We all went into his office, which was quite impressive: oak panelled drinks cabinet, oak table and chairs. "Good morning," said Mr. Hole.

"Good morning," we duly replied.

"You are a load of fraudsters," Mr. Hole suddenly said.

"What are you on about?" replied big Aus, quite sternly.

"This," said Mr. Hole. He then produced two stocks: one we had sanded under the watchful eye of the time and study, and one we had done as usual. "Just compare the two: one is a lot wider than the other – that is, of course, the one you did without the time study." One was certainly wider than the other.

"So, we will in future make sure they are all the same as the one we were timed for," I piped up.

"This is serious! You deliberately spent more time sanding for sanding's sake, when being timed. You could all be dismissed for this," Mr Hole said, threateningly.

At this stage, Ginger and I had to bite our lips, to stop ourselves laughing. We had managed to upset the man at the top, which was a great achievement, considering Mr. Hole thought we were wetting ourselves. But this was the sixties; we had the right to challenge; we had a socialist government. *The Times They Are A-Changing,* I thought to myself.

"What, do you think this is? A circus?" said Mr. Hole, as he banged his fist down on the oak table. Well, I thought, we had brought entertainment to the zoo, and no doubt Mr. Hole fancied himself as the ringmaster. The sooner he realized that the acts wanted more money and better conditions, the sooner we might perform.

"Right, in future time-study doesn't time you lot; you negotiate directly, without the use of the clock," he suddenly said, completely out of the blue. We agreed, and from then onward the sanders, unlike any other group, negotiated direct. We settled our prices and got down to work.

We became real donkeys, as we realized that if we worked really hard, chasing the carrot, we could earn good money. And, that is exactly what we did: we worked and worked, until we achieved the same monies as the car industry. We sweated buckets (Sid sweated oceans). Even though we collapsed when we got home every day, the money was good. We were truly donkeys.

6

Overtime Kills You

Four months had passed and finally The Guns arrived. I was given the choice either to join The Guns in the cage or stop where I was. I decided to stop on the sanding – to the annoyance of Kelly.

By the time I had been in the woodshop for a year, we had increased our numbers. Another Arthur had joined the shop, working on the bench – a fanatic Villa supporter. We called him "Young Arthur", to distinguish him from the older Arthur. Young Arthur was in his forties and a widower.

Another sander had also joined us, a little bloke called Archie, in his early thirties, who suffered from asthma – though that never stopped him getting worked up in an argument; his forefingers could poke you to death in a discussion. As he got angry, so his forefingers would come at you, first his right hand then his left, and as the discussion got deeper, so his fingers became more ferocious. His forefingers could cut any man down to size, no matter his build. He was a man of strong and forceful beliefs, and it was rumoured he had been inside a couple of times. If he was on your side in a debate, argument or come what may, the chances are you would win. His intention in life was to get what he could, and if supporting you helped that, he would be with you, come what may. Most importantly, he believed in the union as the way of securing a better future; in years to come, his support would become invaluable. He had a marvellous ability to cut down responses to: "You reckon? I reckon. You reckon, yeah?"

A recent surprise addition to the shop was a bloke called Dick. He had been employed to work on the machines with David, but as there wasn't enough work he helped all over the place, except sanding. This was a surprise, as there really wasn't enough work for an additional man. He wore an apron, like all other bench hands and machinists, but the difference was that he would never roll up his sleeves, no matter what he was doing or how hot it was. A Geordie in his mid-fifties, his son worked next door in The Guns, under Kelly, and Dick would have his breaks with his son in the Gun Shop.

Dick had an annoying habit of suddenly, without warning, coming onto your job and doing your work, because he was out of work. He also had another annoying habit of coming over to you, starting to speak and then walking off, as he was still speaking.

You could never be sure what he was saying as he walked away, but you always thought it was something nasty. Because of this, he was better known as "Sticky Dicky"; as Eddy would say: "The man's tacky, sticky and a bleeding crawler. Bulls' bollocks, they don't employ people when they haven't got the work! He's got to be a gaffers' man."

The time study was repeatedly coming back to retime David, although he had agreed prices. Every time he was retimed it was to his detriment, and to the benefit of the management. David had managed to keep the machine procedures to himself over the years, but somehow or another time study had sussed him out. His prices were being slashed, as they found out certain operations he was being paid for were not needed. This was not just a threat to his wages, but also a threat to the need and justification of overtime that David thrived on. As the time study cut out more of David's operations, so Sticky Dicky ran out of work. Eventually, dirty Dick became the float, floating all over the shop.

It was a typical Monday morning, with everyone down in the mouth. The time study had just left the shop, after retiming Old Arthur, when I heard Jack shout: "Christ, Mac, get here now!" I ran to the spindle area, thinking there had been an accident. Instead, there was a hell of a fight between Eddy and Sticky Dicky.

Virtually everybody stepped in to stop it. When things cooled down, I spoke to Eddy about the fight. For a man in his sixties to put his job on the line, whatever caused the incident must have been bloody serious. "What caused the fight?" I asked.

"I caught the bugger telling Kelly," he replied.

"Telling him what?"

"How to do the job quicker. It's that bastard who's been grassing on us, bringing in the time study and cutting our wages," he said, forcibly.

Although Kelly wasn't our gaffer, Sticky Dicky often used to speak to him. I thought nothing of it, as his son worked under Kelly. Eddy went on: "Bulls' bollocks, it was Kelly who got him the job! He's a gaffers' man, for Christ's sake."

"Okay Eddy, I'll organize a meeting and we will sort things out, once and for all." I organized the meeting for the next Monday morning at 10.30 a.m. This would give me a week to get things ready, and let things cool down.

That dinnertime, Alfie could be heard telling the two Arthurs and Tom how he had seen David with a woman over the weekend. Alfie's arms were waving and his eyes shining at such revelations.

"I've known David for years. He's a single man; he's never with a woman," said Tom.

"I'm telling you, I saw him with a woman on Saturday in the Bull Ring," argued Alfie.

"What did he say to you?" asked Arthur.

"He didn't; he pretended not to see me and the wife," replied Alfie.

Seeing all the commotion, Eddy walked over and joined the two Arthurs, while I and the sanders listened. "What are you going on about now, Alfie?" asked Eddy.

"David: I saw him with a woman on Saturday, honest," replied Alfie.

"Rubbish! You're gossiping again," said Eddy, nastily. Then, Eddy walked over to where David was having his dinner and asked: "Who was that woman you were with over the weekend?"

"What are you going on about? I was with no woman. Who told you that bullshit?" asked David.

"Alfie's seen you Saturday, in the Bull Ring," replied Eddy, mischievously.

Suddenly in a furious rage, David shuffled off to confront Alfie, and a hell of a row developed, David shouting: "You're not only deaf, you're bloody blind and stupid as well! Don't go round spreading filthy lies about me, you no-good dummy!"

Alfie was having sudden difficulty trying to speak; all he

could do was wave his hands and blink his eyes. While David swore furiously at him, he was pointing with his thumb, as though talking about someone behind him. All this swearing meant nothing to Alfie, just as indeed waving his hands, in a desperate attempt to communicate using sign language, meant nothing to David. I hadn't laughed as much in a long time, and it came as a great relief after the fight earlier.

That Friday night, I attended a branch meeting, as I normally did. The branch meetings were attended by leading shop stewards from the car industry; the branch secretary was a man in his early fifties, known as Fred. He was respected for his honesty and had a reputation for sticking by you through a dispute. I discussed the problem I was experiencing with them, and the advice I received was that the shop get itself organized, to achieve the following: no time study to enter the shop without union permission; nobody to be timed without the shop steward present; nobody employed without our permission; all labour was to come through the union: pre-entry closed shop; to protect our hard-earned wages, we would agree on a ceiling (i.e. nobody would earn above an agreed figure, therefore not ruining the prices and giving the time study a reason for retiming the job); and, finally, no one would work over without union agreement.

Early on the Monday morning of the meeting, I spent time getting the support of the sanders, who knew it would be they, sooner or later, who would have their prices cut. I secured the support of the bench hands, who disliked overtime and those who dragged the work out trying to get it. Then, at 10.30 a.m., I put the proposals to the meeting, emphasizing the need to control the time study and the way people obtained employment. Those two points hit home.

Eddy shouted: "Bloody right! If a bloke ain't in the union then he ain't union-minded and we don't want him. We ain't going to let any more gaffers' men in. Bulls' bollocks to them!"

"Nobody should have to work over; a man should earn enough, or there is something wrong with the job," stated Young Arthur, strongly.

"Time study should never be allowed in the shop. Even if they're only passing through, we should stop work, I reckon," said Archie (also known as "Bren", after the Bren gun, because of the fierceness of his prodding fingers), his forefingers going to and fro.

"I agree entirely about the time study, but the nature of my job – you know, being controlled by the speed of the machines – means I have to work Saturdays to keep all of you going in work," David said, sheepishly.

I wasn't bothered about David's remarks. A number of people would be retiring from the woodshop shortly, and with new union blood there could easily be a shake-up. So, there and then I put it to the meeting that those who had reached the state-registered age for a pension should retire at the next holiday, and all those reaching retirement age in future should retire at their coming holiday. That proposition found no opposition. It was also agreed that anyone found breaking the ceiling should donate the excess amount to a shop fund to be set up. The management were informed of the proposals.

Our demands were met with a peculiar silence. How could they really object? Ceilings meant stability and sensible negotiations; the eradication of overtime meant efficiency; savings would be made by us recruiting all labour. However, management were unlikely to admit this; they were in a state of shock and bewilderment. The shop agreed that we wouldn't take action to achieve these demands; we would take them for granted, and if the management broke any of our proposals, then we would strike.

Within a week, the head of time study came into the shop. We all stopped work and turned off the extractor fan, which brought much welcome silence to the shop. The managers, foremen and the like came running into the shop, to find us all sitting down, making tea and enjoying ourselves. As soon as the bloke left the shop, we started work. Never again did anybody from the time study come into our shop without permission of the union.

The first week after the meeting, no one worked over – even David. The next week, we were approached by management to agree to David working over. A meeting was called and we agreed, as long as management asked us each and every week, which they agreed to.

Within a few weeks, there was talk of new labour coming into shop. We informed management that if labour didn't come through us we would stop work immediately. Management conceded to our demands, on the condition that they had the right to hire and fire. We didn't mind that, as they would have to choose to hire from the labour we would offer them. The management were quick to implement our demands for those who reached retirement age leaving.

The woodshop had demonstrated to the rest of the factory just what could be achieved in a short time, if one organized.

*

Wagger died before he could retire, and David dropped dead on the machines, on a cold November Saturday morning; Sticky Dicky stepped into his job that Monday morning. Jack lost his forefinger six weeks before he was due to retire. Eddy saw retirement, along with Tom and Old Arthur, while Henry retired early with perforated lungs, and died shortly after. The time worked extra for money, by Wagger, David and Henry, was cruelly taken from them, and with much pain. As the years went by, it would seem that only I remembered them.

I attended David's funeral and was stunned to meet a wife and two children, who were beside themselves at his untimely death. Alfie never ever said "I told you so."

7

The Unwelcome and Unplanned Strike Begins

It was 1973, and The Gun Department was now on its own, away from the management control and financial restraints of being part of the Motorcycle Group. In addition, we had a new managing director: Mr. Wales. Previous action to save the motorcycle industry – such as work-ins, fighting redundancy notices, a march through London, meeting leading members of Parliament, and even a protest crowd storming the main building, in what was known as the Golden Mile – had failed to save the company, as a major producer of motorbikes.

I was now married with two young children, and through all the struggles, strikes, work-ins and days away at London, to save the motorbikes and improve our working conditions, my family totally supported me throughout.

We now had our own Works Committee, made up of our own (Guns) shop stewards. I had been elected works convenor and was quite proud of it. We had two unions: T. & G.W.U. (formerly N.U.V.B.: National Union of Vehicle Builders) and the A.E.U. The great thing about having our own identity highlighted was the fact that we were making a profit – although, we knew making a profit and reaping the rewards were two very different things. The lessons learnt from the late '60s and early '70s were: if you were to take on the bosses, then expect a lengthy fight and many a battle.

We were well organized, and had been on many supported marches from Liverpool to London, campaigning against Thatcher and her policies – which were to bring the unions to their knees.

By 1973, we had established a pre-entry closed shop, and decent wages, holidays and conditions, compared to other factories. Mid-1973, we had finalized what we felt was an historic agreement. All production works were piecework – thus, they relied to a degree on the viewers (inspectors), setters and labourers to create continuity of work. The pieceworkers enjoyed the "drift" of increasing monies, while the non-production workers' wages stood still. Therefore, we had agreed with management that all non-production employees (day workers) would be paid a percentage of the pieceworkers' earnings (i.e. setters/toolmakers 100%; viewers 85%; and so on). We had managed to stamp out the bad practices between the pieceworkers and the setters (who would set the machines up for the machinists). Many pieceworkers, at the end of the week, used to give the setter responsible for their machine either fags or money for a drink, fearing that if they didn't the setter would slow the machine down, or just be bloody awkward – such action would affect the amount of production and hence the level of wages for the pieceworker. The agreement would mean it was in the setters' interest to see that production flowed.

3. Marching through London, fighting to protect our union.

My deputy at the time was a bloke called Chitty, of medium height – a pieceworker, and no lover of the setters. He was a machine operator, and represented the largest machine shop. Whenever Chitty spoke to you, he would end up smiling, like his face was on automatic smile mode. He was always one of the first blokes to start work and the last to finish, and was one of those to lose out when we banned overtime working for production workers, earlier in the year, except for emergencies. Banning overtime had a remarkable effect on the conversations people had; they would now talk about The Fonz in *Happy Days*, and there was an urgency to get home to watch early television, which they missed by working over.

We had managed to negotiate with management an extra four days' holiday, by giving up ten minutes of tea break in the afternoon – although, we could continue to make tea in the afternoon. An agreement had been reached for time off with pay, for paternal and bereavement leave. In addition, an equal pay agreement for women had been agreed; we were probably the first in the Midlands to pay women the same as men. The argument which won members over was the belief that, if women were paid the same as men, then the gaffers would prefer to employ men, securing their jobs. Things were slowly developing for the better, so we thought.

However, rumours were flying around that the so-called historic agreement had given the setters a wage above the pieceworkers' average. A meeting was held immediately with Mr. Wales, with Chitty my deputy present.

"Is it true, Mr. Wales?" I asked.

"Why, yes. I negotiated with the A.E.U. rep and agreed to pay setters and toolmakers 115% of the pieceworkers' earnings," he replied.

"But we agreed 100%," I said, forcefully.

"Yes, but I then spoke to their representative, who said quite clearly that he represented them, not you, and we came to an agreement of 115%. And I will honour that agreement."

I replied: "May I remind you that it was I who approached you with this idea, and it was I who held the mass meetings, and got everybody to agree?"

Wales argued: "You may well have done, but you never held meetings with the setters, did you?"

"No, I didn't; I don't represent them. They are in the A.E.U. But I am the works convenor and the A.E.U. recognize that fact – as indeed do you yourself. At least I believed that you did."

"Yes I did, and I do, but I was of the understanding that the Works Committee had agreed," replied Wales.

"Well, you were wrong, and such action – and I reiterate – will lead to a strike. Will you therefore agree to suspend its implementation, until this whole matter is sorted out?" I said, forcibly.

"I will only say that I will see the A.E.U. rep and consider what you say," he replied.

The whole maddening thing about all this is that we'd had discussions with the A.E.U. from the start, and they fully agreed to the original agreement. As I walked down the stairs from his office to the production area, Chitty said: "Bloody hell, Mac. The lads won't wear this, and they won't believe we didn't know about it."

I responded: "We will have a meeting straight away with all the stewards, and give Wales time to sort things out. The last thing we want at the moment is a strike." As I walked through Chitty's shop, to call all the stewards to a meeting, I could see the lads flocking to Chitty, to see what was going on. We held our meeting in what was known as the "stewards' office" (also known as the "Hut"), a dirty old room at the end of the building; at a tight squeeze, all the stewards could just about get in. I informed them of what was going on, and made it clear that if we went on strike immediately we would be fighting on two fronts: the A.U.E. and management.

Chitty got up from his chair, arguing: "We won't be able to stop the lads. They won't stand for those bloody setters getting fifteen per cent more." He then paused momentarily, his facing rearranging into a smile.

Abdul, a leading shop steward representing another machine shop, spoke in his normal manner (when he spoke seriously, it was as though he was going to cry); "I think Mac is right: if we go on strike right now, without going back to management, we will never know whether we could have avoided going on strike."

Fortunately, they agreed with me. As I walked from the stewards' office (Hut) back to my own shop, to tell them in the woodshop what was going on, I could see people stopping work and going to Chitty. I had just informed my lads in the woodshop, when in walked Chitty and said: "They're going home, Mac. They won't listen; they're on strike." I walked with Chitty into his shop, to find he was right: his shop was deserted.

I immediately rung Wales. "Mr. Wales, have you agreed to suspend the agreement? The lads are hostile to it."

Wales replied: "You have already caused a strike? But you agreed to let me consider the situation! The agreement stands."

"You don't realize the strength against this. Only the main machine shop has gone home as yet; no others – a full-scale strike can still be averted," I replied, earnestly.

"No. I shall honour my agreement; the setters will receive 115%," he responded, forcefully. "I learnt some time ago that one should never break agreements; if you do, people lose all respect for you, and you are thus weakened as a negotiator."

A mass meeting was called of those remaining, where I put it to them that Wales would not move and the main machinists had gone home. My advice, therefore, was that we had no alternative but to join them in striking. It was unanimously agreed and we all walked out.

8

The First Casualty of the Strike: The Milkman

Nothing really happened the first week; Wales ignored us and paid the setters 115% for doing nothing, while we suffered on strike. The Sunday after the first week on strike, the stewards met in the Piled Arms Club in Small Heath, and agreed to a full-scale picket. Going on strike instantly, the way we had, took from us the advantage of planning – we were now to put that right. The works opened at 7.30 a.m. for production workers and 8.00 a.m. for white-collar staff; pickets would be there for 6.45 a.m.

    Being keen, I was on the picket duty at 6.00 a.m. on my own; it was my belief that you had to lead from the front, not from behind. I hadn't wanted to strike, but the lads had, and I was going to do my damnedest to win. I was at the entrance to the works, and the large gates (nicknamed the "Berlin Gates") were still closed. The road leading to the works was straight and came off a busy main road. I looked straight down the road, with its back-to-back houses on the right and the old motorcycle works stretched down the other. I stood there alone, willing to take anybody on.

And there, coming up the road, was my first challenge: the milkman. As he drove up to the gates, I stepped out in front of him. The milkman shouted: "How many do you want? Past or Stera?"

"Neither. We are on strike here," I replied.

"It's alright, mate, I'm only delivering milk."

"Well, I'm asking you not to, or you will be crossing a picket line."

He looked left, then right, then all around and said: "Where's the bleeding picket line?"

"At the moment, I'm it; it's still early. And I'm asking you not to cross the picket line."

"How on Earth is me delivering milk gonna help or hinder your strike? Beats me," he replied, sarcastically.

"That's not the point; no one should cross the picket line. Anyhow, delivering milk gives them sustenance. But, they'll be choked if they see even the milkman is showing solidarity with us."

He seemed to consider this point. "Okay, I'm in the union myself; I won't cross it," he replied.

I was dead chuffed. It had been worth getting there for 6.00 a.m.: I had successfully stopped someone. By 6.45 a.m. there were over a hundred pickets – easily enough to stop anyone getting through. At 7.00 a.m., when the early birds arrived for work, the shock on the setters' faces was quite something, when they saw we were there first.

9

They Are All Scabs Now

For a whole week, the setters had gone to work with nothing to do, on full pay. Now they were to become official scabs, to enable them to continue. As the setters started appearing, their numbers increased. In amongst the setters were two machinists, heads bowed, who should have been on strike with the rest of us – but they had been secretly scabbing.

The two lads were from Redditch. One was in his late forties and the other in his late twenties. The older bloke was George and the younger was known as "Fat Arse" – most of us never knew his true name, but wherever he worked his arse got in the way, hence he was called "Fat Arse". The pickets were in a rage to think that these two, who had been the first to walk out, were scabbing. This made the pickets more determined than ever not to let anyone through

It was just before 8.00 a.m., and the staff had yet to arrive. The setters had swelled in numbers to thirty-odd. Now they assembled and charged the pickets. As they met the pickets' resistance, they kicked them where it hurt. The air was blue with the language. One stocky bloke known as "Barn" seemed to be enjoying charging the pickets; his card was marked. On the third charge, the machine scabs managed to get through, to the steps leading to their workplace, before they were jumped on by at least two pickets, who dragged them away, shouting and kicking. The hate for those two scabs was greater than that for the setters. The line reformed and the breach was repaired.

As the staff arrived in their cars, we refused to let them in. They would usually park their cars on the premises, as the road itself was only just wide enough for cars to pass, so this caused a traffic jam, right back to the main road and beyond. The staff were clearly embarrassed, not knowing what to do. As my deputy, Chitty often said: "They had everything given to them. They have never fought for anything, and thus don't know the value of anything." We certainly did, and we were fighting for it. Bewildered and bemused, they just stood there by their cars, not knowing what to do.

Eventually, Wales turned up (by now, The Guns' works manager Hole had gone home). "Good morning, Mac. Would you please remove the pickets and let me through?"

"Yes, of course I will; if you will remove the fifteen per cent extra you have given the setters – or better still, give everyone else fifteen per cent extra – I will gladly remove the pickets," I replied.

"Look here, you know my position, now let me through," he said, with the air of royalty.

For the first time, us workers felt on equal terms; we did not have to do anything we didn't want to do. It was a glorious feeling, almost like the chains of being part of the working class had been ripped off of us by the gaffer's weakest link: the right to strike. He was ignored and no one was getting through.

Within ten minutes, the police arrived. "Who is in charge?" a policeman yelled.

"I am," I said.

At that, he grabbed me, along with another officer, and pushed me up against the wall, making it clear that he did not like what was going on. "Right, you little bastard! I don't want a Grunwick (a dispute which lasted for two years and had national media coverage) here, and I am not going to have one. Do you understand?"

I refused to answer; I had now seen the side of the police normally talked about by the far left of the union. As his clutched hand let go of my clothing, about a dozen police officers arrived.

It didn't take them long to escort the scabs into work. But the pickets knew the police presence would diminish to nought at the end of the day.

By two in the afternoon, the picket numbers diminished and the police presence disappeared. Scores were now to be settled. We all disappeared by 2.30, leaving them believing they were safe.

The next morning we appeared in strength; no one could get in. What's more, only two policemen had turned up, after scuffles broke out between us and the scabs. The policemen had a different philosophy this time: they tried talking things through. They made it quite clear that we would have to let in those who wanted to go in.

As the machine scabs went in, they were taunted with remarks such as, "You will have a sweet 'Fat Arse' when we're finished with you," and, "George, you're dead." Bren taunted: "You still gotta come out yet!" This was somehow made to rhyme: *"You wanna get in, you've gotta get out!"* The chanting was horrendous.

At eleven o'clock, the manager Mr. Black came out, saying the scab machinists had gone home. "They managed to get across the canal, go round the back of you all and get into George's car and away," Mr. Black stated. The pickets ran down the road to find that George's car had indeed gone. There was an almighty cheer; after two days picketing we had marked up a success.

It was now 4.30 p.m. on the second day of picketing, and most pickets had hung on to the end, to goad the scabs as they went home. With so many pickets still there at the end of the day, it would be more difficult for the scabs to get out than it was to get in. The setters slowly came out of the factory, into their cars, which management had allowed them to park alongside the buildings. The setters received the expected chants of "scabbing bastards!" Then Barn came out and things went quiet; every picket's eyes were on him. As he got into his car and drove slowly toward the pickets, his car seemed to jump, then swayed and careered. The pickets roared with laughter. "What's wrong, tough guy? Run out of wind? Or is it his guts, I reckon?" shouted Bren. All of Barn's tyres were flat. He stopped the car and ran back into the factory. Black then came out to find the pickets still laughing, with Bren saying, as clear as daylight: "Found some wind then, I reckon." We all left, knowing that someone had settled a score by slashing every tyre on his car.

I got home that night hoping that Wales would realize the feelings of those on strike, now entering a second week without money. And, hopefully, he would lay off the setters until the matter had resolved itself. If the setters were laid off, then the A.U.E. would have an interest in settling the dispute.

And the next day – Wednesday – it happened: Wales laid off all the setters at 10.00 a.m., to the cheers of the pickets. We were now all in the same boat, but the difference was we had fought for everything, and they – the setters – had been given everything. We were certainly in the same boat, but if the boat capsized we could swim; they would most certainly drown. Well, that may have been what I believed. But they paddled on.

By the third week of the strike, we had got into a routine: I would be there at seven o'clock, along with Young Arthur (now known as "Fatty Arthur") and his mate Sam, an Irishman, who was the sprayer from the machine shop.

At 7.15 a.m. Chitty would arrive, followed by Mick from the woodshop. He had a crop of curly, black hair, and after every word he spoke would say, "O"; so, where we would say, "Good day," he would say, "Good day O," and almost everyone was called "Kid O." He was a very likeable lad, in his late twenties. Sam was often called "Telegram Sam", after his favourite singer Mark Bolan. From dinnertime, others would join the line. By now, the pickets had got the Berlin Gates to work, which enabled them to shut the gates and only open them when they wished to.

Wales would drive up to the gates and get out, open the gates and carry on in, after a tussle with the pickets. So, the daily routine was to hold the remaining scabs (staff) up as much as possible.

It was Monday in the third week of the strike, and it was bucketing down. Then, up drove Wales in his car. He called me over to his car, wound the window down and said: "Open the gate for me please, Mac."

"Open it yourself," I replied, which he did, getting drowned in the process. By now, the staff were continually going in, along with two maintenance men: an electrician and fitter. Always with the same excuse: "We wish we could join you, but we're not in the same union." This was quite rich coming from an electrician, as he drove his new Ford through the gates, along with Wales in his Rover 3000. After watching them going in, Bren said: "We're daft. Why don't we paint the handle on the gates just before they arrive, and then it will go all over the cars' interior and exterior? What do you reckon?" Next morning, when they were seen turning into the road, we painted the underside of the handles. We watched as they moved the handles, then as they drove off, with paint all over the interior of their cars. Neither the electrician nor Wales bothered to speak to us again on the picket line.

The third week was a rather exciting week for the pickets, for the management had engaged the services of a carpet fitter. Obviously, the management weren't expected to work on bare concrete floors or walk on bare steps; they must have carpet. By now, most delivery vehicles had stopped delivering, and that included Royal Mail. Then, out of the blue, a van appeared at the gate. Fatty Arthur approached the van and said, in his polite manner: "Sorry, mate, official picket line – please don't cross it."

The bloke in his mid-thirties replied: "I've got nothing to do with the strike. I'm just going to lay some carpets."

"Sorry, mate, they can't afford lino, let alone carpet; there's a strike on," said Fatty Arthur.

At this, the van driver grew agitated. "I've signed a contract to lay carpets and I'm going to," he replied, aggressively.

"I've signed a contract of employment and it's been broken – so what?" Arthur replied.

At that, the driver wielded a very large spanner at Arthur and drove on. By the time the driver got out of his van to enter the factory, a large crowd of pickets had arrived. Wielding the large spanner, he made his way into the factory. The pickets were now very concerned by his attitude; Bren said, fiercely: "That will cost him, I reckon!" That afternoon, a number of pickets stayed on late, waiting for the carpet man (carpet bagger). At 5.30 he left the building, his van swaying, jumping and careering all over the place; his tyres had been slashed. After that, he continued crossing the picket line, but was now apologizing for doing so. He was there seven working days, and his tyres were slashed on three occasions.

As well as the carpet layer upsetting the pickets by his actions, a number of staff had also upset them. One French woman in particular had remarked "Bollocks" to Telegram Sam. From that moment on she was called the "French wanker", which horrified staff and police. The police visited the picket line on numerous occasions, about the use of such bad language. The pickets really thought this humorous: such words as "le French wanker" had caused more upset on the picket lines than anything else! The pickets were really hitting home now! As Bren said, tongue in cheek: "We were asked to mind our French."

10

Nice Countryside Trip to Kidderminster

The strike was in its fifth week, cash was tight and we were all suffering; I had a wife and two young children. But, if I was finding it hard, God-knew how Mick O was managing, with four! I had received no money from the Social, for myself or the family – apparently, Mrs. Thatcher had decided I was not entitled to any. Unfortunately, my Social Services office was in a place called Kidderminster, at least eighteen miles from the picket line. So, I arrived at 7.00 a.m. on the picket line, to leave at ten for an appointment at the Social in Kidderminster, at 10.45. There was not much going on at the picket line, so Fatty Arthur said: "Come on, I'll go with you; be a nice day out, driving through the countryside."

As Arthur got into the car, I warned him: "Careful you don't hit your head when we go round corners; this is a three-wheeler, not a Rolls." We drove across the city, bouncing as we went, with Arthur sitting snug and generally acting as if I was his chauffeur.

As we left the city and hit the countryside, the ride became more pleasant – until, of course, we hit the road from Bromsgrove to Kidderminster, known as the Kidderminster Road. The road was like a lengthy snake, feeling as if the moment you come out of one bend you hit another. The plastic pig hit the first bend and there was a loud noise.

"What was that bang?" Arthur shouted.

"My head!" I confirmed. As soon as we entered another bend, there was another bang... pause... bang. "You never been in a plastic pig before, Arthur?"

"No, and I don't want to again," he said, as he sat rigid in his seat.

"Come on, Arthur, it gets you from A to B. We've almost arrived."

"Yes, but not in one piece. I feel like I've been ten rounds with Cassius Clay, only I would have been paid for that!" he said, half-jokingly.

The road began to straighten out as we got closer to Kidderminster. As we drove into the town centre, I asked Arthur to look out for a place to park. As we passed the Social Services offices, Arthur shouted: "Park there, alongside the offices." Arthur was impatient to get out of the car – not so much because of the car ride, but because he was generally nosey, and curious to see what would happen to me in Social Services. I drove around again and he repeated: "Just in front; you can park there."

"No, there's a yellow line," I replied.

"Yes, but it doesn't matter; others are parking there," he said.

"So they are," I replied. So, I was able to park the car almost right alongside Social Services. We entered the building and made our way up the stairs, to the relevant area. The room itself was shaped something like a cinema, with rows of chairs looking down at the reception. You just sat down and waited your turn, then when someone got up and left in front of you, you took their place. We were there about forty minutes, but a very interesting forty minutes.

In front was a family: a husband, wife and two children, aged about seven and ten. In front of them was a man in corduroy trousers, sat on his own. We could quite clearly hear all that was going on. The man in cords got up went to the hatch. "Good morning," he said to the woman on the other side of the hatch, "I have run out of money, and I need to put central heating into the house I have bought and am renovating. I wondered if you would be so kind as to help with the financial arrangements." The woman on the other side of the hatch informed him of the relevant forms to fill in, and off he went. Arthur turned, smiled at me and nodded, saying: "You'll be alright here, Mac."

The two children were busily engaged in looking through some *Butlin's* brochures; the little one was waving one of the brochures and pointing at a page; "Mummy, Mummy can we go?" The little girl then went to her dad, doing the same. The father smiled, looked at the brochure and replied: "Soon as we have got the money from here, we'll go to one – or both."

Arthur again looked at me, smiled and said: "You'll be more than alright here, Mac. See that bloke to get your central heating done, then see that family for a holiday, while your central heating is being done. There you go, Mac." We both just laughed.

After, on leaving the building, we saw there was a traffic warden about to place a ticket on my car. "Hold on, there's been a mistake," I said, calmly. "I am not familiar with the area and saw others parking here, so I thought I was alright."

"Are you disabled?" he asked.

"No," I replied.

"You ain't alright, then," he stated, sharply.

Smiling at this, Arthur joked: "Well, he is alright if he's not disabled."

"To be parked here you can't be alright; you must be

disabled," the traffic warden replied.

"I do apologize, but I'm not working – that's why I've come to Social Services," I said.

"What are you doing owning and running a car if you're unemployed, then?" he said, sarcastically.

"Well, it's temporary unemployment, in reality. What I mean is that I'm out on strike and I haven't had any money for five weeks – that's why I'm here," I said, calmly.

With that, the traffic warden looked at me, and his look said everything: *You're the enemy from within – a communist. You lot ought to be shipped to Russia. You don't want to work. You're a Bolshie.* At that, he slapped the ticket into my hand. Arthur just gave a half-smile.

I was informed by Social that I would get a fiver; the parking ticket cost a fiver. I could sense that Arthur was keen to get back to the picket line to tell the others what had happened, and this he did with enthusiasm and clarity.

11

Not Just a Battle, But a War

It was about 2.30 p.m. on the picket line. The carpet fitter had gone out for lunch; he had been sticking fingers up at us and waving money at us. This had really upset Mick O, who was finding it hard to survive, with his family of four young children. "I'll have that bastard," said Micko.

Micko had gone off at about 12.30 p.m. and returned at 2.00 p.m. – he had obviously been drinking, though no one knew where he got the money from. He had walked eight miles to get to the picket line that morning.

At 2.30 p.m. the carpet man returned from lunch to find the gates closed, so he stopped to get out of his van. "You stupid, lazy bastards," he said, walking across to open the gate. He then drove through and parked up. That was when I gave the signal to form a picket line across the road, stopping him and his mates from getting in. After five weeks on strike without a penny, no one had buried the hatchet in respect of his previous gestures and taunts.

The carpet man (or the "carpet bagger", as the lads called him) stood at 6'2", with a slim, athletic build. As he tried to force his way through, chanting, "You lazy, no-good bastards," Micko appeared with an axe; the taunts and gestures he had made were just too much for Micko, whose wife and children were suffering because of an injustice. The carpet bagger gestured and taunted, like so many had before him, knowing that the pickets wouldn't hit back, for fear of prosecution. But, as Micko went at him with the axe, caught in the middle of the pickets, the fear of God hit him.

"Christ's sake!" he shouted, as Bren and Arthur grabbed Micko. The pickets eased off and the carpet bagger moved back, shouting: "Get that axe off the stupid bugger!" Then he looked at me, frantically; "Do something, will you?!"

I just looked at Micko, who was shouting at him: "Still want to cross the picket line? Just bloody try."

I looked at the carpet bagger and said: "Well, do you?"

The carpet bagger replied: "You think you're tough with the axe, don't you?"

"Mick, drop the axe," I said, which Micko did, before squaring up to the carpet bagger.

"Right," I shouted to the carpet bagger, "now you can try and come through."

The carpet bagger went to his van, his mates having already retreated. As he turned the van around to drive off, he shouted: "I've finished the job anyway, and I never really wanted to cross the picket line." We never saw him again.

Micko, although the worse for drink, had injected life and fulfilment into the picket line – the strike was now more than just a battle; it was a war! We were fighting for what was right and just. We had no money, were broke and on the verge of starvation but, with our families' support, we were prepared to starve, rather than give in. Years of being beholden to the setters was over; we had fought over decades for better conditions, and we were certainly not going to be subservient to a group of people because they were classed as "skilled", while we were considered second rate, being only "semi-skilled". The days of women crying and men worried to death that they might upset the setter, thus not being able to earn their wages, were over. The dispute would put both setters and management in their place.

That afternoon, we had a meeting of the pickets. In my rallying speech, I said: "The management have their own canteen, their own entrance, their own parking places and their company cars. No clocking in for them, they don't have a half-hour dinner break; their dinners take two hours. They have to have special parking places, because they get in late and go home early. They even have to have separate toilets, because they discharge differently to us. Because the directors are so busy, they are unable to be on the premises for too long, and they have to have other people helping them, which they call 'managers' – and, of course, those directors who are the busiest, and thus aren't here often, have to have the most managers, to do the work for them. And, of course, those with the most managers have the most responsibility, because they're never here, so they receive the most money. And, because they come into work two hours after the production workers, managers also have to have a parking place, and their own toilet and eating place.

"For the art of managing is to never get dirty, and always be seen in a collar and tie. Hence, they cannot sit where we have sat, in relation to eating or discharging. The management deals with the director and thus is privileged, hence he or she must be careful who he or she is talking to, or he or she will lose their awesomeness. Therefore, he or she has people below them, who can talk to us plebs in a language we understand, who can check at any time where we are, by entering the toilets, telling us how long a discharge takes and how often we should have one. Who checks what time we came in by looking at our clocking-in cards, but of course doesn't clock in. And yes, of course, he or she has their own toilet. Then, of course, the foremen need people to watch our every move. People who use the same canteen, toilet, have to park their cars where they can and, of course, clock in: 'setters'. We, of course, are not allowed to set our own machines, as that would make the job too interesting; we are left to sweat every minute of the day, operating machines and expecting them to do miracles, called 'programmes'. The setters have a responsibility to see that machines are set and ready for use – that is, ready for us to work like idiots. And for that they get fifteen per cent more.

"So, let's weigh it up: the directors do the least and get the most; the managers do slightly more, so they get slightly less than the directors, but more than the foreman, who gets less than the managers, for doing slightly more. And the setters get slightly less than the foreman, but more than the production worker, though it's the production worker who produces the products that create the wealth."

I concluded: "This dispute is about fairness, equality and, most of all, justice. there is no justice in us, the producers of wealth, receiving less than those we carry."

At that, we took a vote, and unanimously decided to carry on.

12

Resolution in Sight

We were now eight weeks into the strike. Every two weeks we held a meeting and took a vote to carry on. It was in the eighth week that I was told by my outside organizer – a Mr. Silver – that Mr. Wales wanted to see me. It was the Thursday before the fortnightly Friday on which we held our meeting, as to whether we continued or not.

The word got round to everybody that we had a meeting organized, and expectations were high. At ten o'clock that Thursday morning, myself and Chitty went up the stairs to Wales's office, leaving the lads on the picket duty. On the way, Chitty said: "Well, Mac, what do to think he's going to offer?"

"No idea. I just hope we have got something to tell the lads tomorrow," I replied.

We were ushered into the conference room. It was quite a strange feeling to be back inside the plant while on strike. Wales walked in with his financial director, Mr. Wax, and opened up the meeting by saying: "Gentlemen, it's ridiculous you carrying on with the dispute. You are ruining the reputation of the company and putting your own jobs in jeopardy."

"Mr. Wales, I haven't come here today to discuss who is or isn't ruining the company; I have come here expecting a fruitful discussion. If it's not going to be constructive then I will leave now," I replied.

Wales tapped his fingers on the table and replied: "This dispute has nothing to do with me; it is the A.U.E. you have the dispute with. I suggest you meet with them and sort your problems out."

"It was *you* we made the agreement with, and *you* who made what were obviously two conflicting agreements: one with us and one with the A.E.U. – and now you are honouring theirs and not ours," I replied.

"Well, all I can say is I'm not budging. Therefore, you should tell your men to call off the strike," he stated.

"I will inform them tomorrow," I replied. Then Chitty and I left the room.

On the way down the stairs, Chitty said: "What do we tell the lads? Christ, they were expecting something." His face then turned into its well-rehearsed grin, but Chitty was worried.

"We tell them the truth: it took eight weeks before he sat down with us, only to tell us to return to work."

We informed the pickets and prepared ourselves for the mass meeting the next day.

The mass meeting was well attended. It began at eleven o'clock around the gates; this made the area secure, ensuring that nothing went in or out of the factory. There was an expectation in the air that something was on offer. After informing the meeting of financial contributions that had been made by a number of union branches, and how we were to distribute the money, I informed them of the outcome of the meeting with Wales.

"He tells us – instructs us – to return to work and call off the strike, because he says so; we are ruining the company and jeopardizing our jobs. This from a man who rarely comes in on a Monday, because it coincides with him playing golf. Look in his car on a Tuesday: his golf clubs are still there, in case he's called to the golf club again. This from a man who employs managers, foremen and setters, because he is incapable of running the company on his own. We, the production workers, along with the labourers, packers and viewers, produce the profits which allow him the privilege of playing golf on Mondays. Who afford him a company car, in which he misses the rush hour, by coming in late and going home early.

"We will not return with our tails between our legs, but with our heads held high, with the battle won. It's taken him eight weeks to meet us, yet if he doesn't want to settle, then why see us at all? The settlement is in his hands, not ours; the making of the dispute was his, as is its resolution. We will not go back with our tails between our legs."

The vote result was unanimously to continue the strike. Wales's ultimatum gave us a welcome opportunity to give him our official reply, which we planned to do the following Monday. We could, of course, have told him that on Friday, but he would know by Friday afternoon, and if he was bluffing he had the weekend to sweat it out. Bill and I informed our outside organizer, and arranged to see Wales on Monday at two o'clock – which would, of course, upset his golfing; the pickets loved the idea.

We were cockahoop that Monday, walking up the stairs to the conference room. Chitty remarked: "What do you think he will say when you tell him?"

"Couldn't give a damn, to tell you the truth. After eight weeks, the lads are solid. Wales has got a problem; he is in trouble and he knows it," I answered. We did have some fun, ruining as best we could the new carpet laid on the stairs.

We entered the conference room to find Wales already in there, sat between Black and Wax. Wales looked like he was being propped up (sloshed, I thought). As I told him the lads' reply, his face changed colour. He just replied: "Thank you and good day." Although we had nothing to report back to the lads, at least we could impart his physical appearance, which informed us that we were onto a winner.

That afternoon, we were informed by our organizer Mr. Silver that there was to be a meeting the next day, Tuesday, at two o'clock. He would be there, along with the A.E.U., to meet Wales, to try to get to an agreement; Chitty and I would also be there.

As Chitty and I walked up those stairs once again, to the conference room, I remarked to Chitty: "No matter what, we do not budge a thou – not a thou."

"Great stuff," Bill replied, and his face turned into a big grin.

We all met in the conference room, along with our organizers. Norman (A.U.E. steward) had his own organizer: a bloke called Duffy, of slim build and medium height, who sounded like he smoked a lot. Wales informed us that he was prepared to call in ACAS, if we agreed. As far as I was concerned, I had little problem with that idea, and an ACAS representative duly arrived the next day.

Chitty and I were in one room, and Norman with his organizer in the other. The ACAS bloke just kept going from one room to the other, trying to find grounds to settle. After three hours, the ACAS bloke asked if I would be prepared to have a discussion with the A.U.E., without the management and without anybody else there. Chitty and I agreed.

As we waited for Norman and Duffy to come into the conference room, I remarked to Chitty: "Don't forget, we don't budge an inch."

"You're right," he replied, and his face turned into a grin.

Norman and Duffy came into the room, then Duffy immediately started saying: "You're on good numbers here. Why do you want to spoil it? You're better off than most. For goodness' sake, just call it a day and look after your jobs."

I felt this was pathetic talk. *Is that all he's got to offer?* I thought. So, I let him have it. "Yes, we're on good numbers, but no thanks to you lot: you have never joined us in the past, in any fight we have had. You bloody lot still wanted to carry on working over, causing machine breakdowns so that you would work Saturdays. All you have ever done is cling to our backs, and now you cheeky sods are trying to jump from our shoulders and trample on us. Well, unlike you lot, we fought for what we got. To us it's a war; this is just one of the battles."

At this, Duffy took out his inhaler, coughing and wheezing – I had set the poor bloke off. Chitty looked at me and smiled. After regaining his breath, Duffy responded: "You're a maniac. You'll lose everyone their jobs. You have got to be sensible."

I replied: "I'm sensible, alright. Why should we work bloody hard for you lot to receive fifteen per cent more? Get stuffed. If we have to close the company we will do it."

"I don't want to," he replied, "but it looks like I will have to be the one to save the company. You don't know a good number when you have one."

"Come on, Chitty, let's get back to the picket line, where we can do some good," I said, menacingly. We left the room with Duffy gasping for air and Norman looking stunned.

On the way down the stairs, Chitty remarked: "Christ, you're hard, Mac. He might have settled."

"Settled? You mean compromised. We are not compromising, after losing eight weeks. The man Duffy will settle," I replied. Unfortunately, this time Chitty did not smile; he was obviously weakening.

We reported to the pickets, who were proud of our stance. It was becoming obvious to me that a saying reiterated to me by an old campaigner, Freddy Elliot, who had organized many disputes in the late fifties and sixties, was coming true; "It's easier to take them out than it is to get them back." How right he was. You could promise the world, but you could rarely deliver it. I informed the pickets that I expected Wales would be getting in touch with us.

All this movement and no settlement was psychologically affecting us all. Every time we went to a meeting expectations were high, only to be knocked down again when we got nowhere.

Then, the breakthrough came.

Wales wanted to see us on Friday at two o'clock. No remarks were made going up the stairs this time; we were on edge. We were all there in the conference room – myself, Chitty, Mr. Silver, Norman and Duffy – when Wales walked in with Wax. Wales opened up by saying: "I have tried to come up with an offer that I hope both sides would agree upon. Mr. Duffy assures me the setters will accept 100% of the average production workers' pay, and it will be reviewed every six months – not yearly, as present. I hope this will be agreed, and will be the end of the matter."

"Will the other day workers' wages be reviewed every six months?" I asked. "Labourers, packers, viewers?"

"No, just setters," he replied, then left the meeting.

My question had caused Duffy to go for his inhaler. After regaining his breath, he said: "The setters have given up a lot to settle this dispute. I hope you realize that fact."

"They have given it up because they never had to fight for it in the beginning," I replied.

On the way out, our outside organizer Mr. Silver said: "Well done, you can't get anything better; accept it."

Chitty agreed; "We have won. Come on, Mac: agree." By now, you couldn't stop Chitty smiling again.

"Leave it up to the day workers whether they will accept the setters getting a review every six months, which could well end up with them getting a rise."

We agreed to call a mass meeting the coming Monday, at eleven o'clock; over the weekend, I would contact the day-work stewards to see what they thought. Not one day worker was against the agreement; this trend was repeated at the mass meeting.

So, on Tuesday, we returned to work, after nine weeks on strike, our heads held high and kings of the roost. The resounding cheers of delight when the strike was over can never be forgotten. The lads and lasses had had their summer holidays ruined, all their savings were used up and bills were outstanding. The cheers were of delight but, most of all, relief.

13

A Burning Issue

Of all the things that had been achieved over the years, there was still nowhere to rest from the dust of the stocking shop (woodshop). The only break was when the extractor fan was turned off, which was met with peace and tranquillity. No noise meant no work, which meant we could have a cup of tea, a smoke or just a rest. Pull a chair out from beside you your bench/machine, sit down and have a brew – amongst the dust, dirt and rubbish created through work. When the fan was switched back on, push the chair back, along with your cup, and work on to the next break. Of course, the foreman had an office big enough to seat everyone from the stocking shop.

If you smoked (most people in the shop smoked), you had to go outside by the toilet at break, along with your cup of tea. There was no place for the workers; only those who watched the workers had a room.

Kelly (now our gaffer) had his office in the stocking shop,

which he took over from Matthews when he retired. "Don't worry," I said, "they're putting an office up in Gun Assembly, next door; he'll be moving soon."

"Moving?" said Arthur. "They ought to move him for good – into his grave."

Noticing we were talking about something, Sticky Dicky walked over. "What you on about? Kelly moving?"

"Yes, the sooner he moves out, the better," I said.

"Kelly was telling my boy they're going to use his office as a storeroom when he moves out," Sticky Dicky went on to say.

"Storeroom?" popped up Derek, from the back of the bench. "How about a rest room?"

"I reckon you're right. What you reckon, Mac?" Bren said, with a smile on his face.

"I'll have a go; don't see why not. We've got nowhere away from the dust to eat. Yes, I'll have a go."

"'Rest room' is right: a rest from his idiot ranting. And, at the speed he walks through the shop to get to his office, he'll cause a fire. We should be left alone, without that barking Kelly popping up all over the place," said Arthur.

I realized then that I had to achieve Kelly's office as the woodshop's rest room. If we could achieve it, then all the other polluted shops would soon follow.

At that time, Dago – a tall, slim lad in his mid-twenties – had joined us. He had just finished a fire marshal course. The gaffer had agreed to give those who completed the course fifty pounds a year to be the company's fire officers – not a bad deal, thought Dago. In the event of a real fire, his duty was to call in the professionals. Dago and myself, along with two others, had also gone on a first aid course. Unfortunately, they were held of an evening, over a six-week period, although once having gained the St. John's certificate, the gaffer gave you another fifty quid for being the shop's first aider. Of course, being the works convenor I declined the fifty quid. As far as fire training is concerned, I had picked up a bit on trade union courses. We had an asset in Dago; if he felt there was a fire danger in the woodshop, he would empty the woodshop of people and investigate. Just such an investigation happened after we had finished discussing Kelly's office.

"Mac," shouted Rob, who worked on the bandsaw, alongside his brother Jim on the crosscut saw (they had both replaced the old-timers), "I can smell burning!" Jim was slim, of average height, and reminded me of a "spiv", like the wheeler-dealer in *Dad's Army*. His brother was slightly older, fat and always smiling; they were both well-experienced wood machinists. "You had better come over here and smell."

I walked over, along with his brother Jim. "You can smell it, alright," I said. I knew that Rob smoked at his workplace at break times, hidden behind the bandsaw. "Dago," I shouted, "you're needed! Looks like something's burning."

"Leave everything alone," he replied, and came over like a flash. "Yeah, something's burning; it's coming from under the ducting. This could be dangerous: once the air gets to it, it could explode, with all that dust around," Dago said, seriously. He walked over to Sticky Dicky. "Turn the extractor off; I think we have a fire."

Sticky Dicky turned the extractor fan off, and Dago informed everyone but me to leave the shop while he investigated.

The other fire marshal from the machine shop joined us, as Dago gave instructions. "This is what we'll do: Mac, you lift the ducting cover up from the floor; Dave, you turn the water on and I will point the hose at the source of the fire. Hopefully, nothing will explode," he added, with confidence.

"Hold on, Dago, if it's that dangerous shouldn't we call the professionals in? After all, that's what you always say," I pointed out to him.

"What, and let them find a load of Rob's stub-ends behind the bandsaw? Come on, nothing will happen if we're ready," he said, once again with confidence.

The ducting covers were made of wood and approximately five feet long. It soon dawned on me that, if there was to be an explosion, it would no doubt be in a ball of fire – and it was me who would be in the firing line. However, as I was works convenor, I couldn't show weakness; I had to do it.

"Okay, Mac, I'll count to five then lift it."

"Okay, gotcha," I replied.

"Five, four, three, two, one," shouted Dago.

I lifted the panel, and there in the dust was a snaking flame – like a fuse burning along the dust, just where Rob sat at break times. The hose was turned on, spraying water at the source.

"Lift the next panel – quick, Mac," Dago shouted. "God knows how far it's gone." As quick as lightning I lifted the panel, as Dago soaked the ducting. Five panels were lifted before we got to the end of the flame burning away; as each panel was lifted I feared an explosion, and I was more than relieved when it was over. There was little doubt that, had the smouldering gone on for much longer, the woodshop would have gone up in smoke, with one mighty explosion.

Mr. Black walked into the shop. "Everything alright? Under

control?"

"It is now," Dago replied. "The dust had been smouldering for ages; it had almost got to the Gigor…" (some thirty feet away) "…then the whole place would have gone up."

Black looked carefully along the ducting, to where Rob worked. "Who sits here?" he asked.

"It's irrelevant who sits here," I replied; "the fact is the ducts shouldn't have dust in them; they should be regularly inspected and cleaned out. Management's neglect has put my members' lives in danger."

Black froze, realizing that what I said had some truth in it. "I will see to this immediately," he said, and walked off.

Rob then appeared. "Okay, can I get back to work now? No more burning issues smouldering away, lads?"

"The only burning issue is that it started where you sit for your breaks and have a smoke," I replied.

"Come off it! If I have the odd fag, I always make sure they are out. What a state of affairs, when you blame the bloke who reported the fire for starting it! Next time I'll let the place burn down, if that's all the thanks I get. Most places give you a fiver for reporting a fire; here you get accused and maligned. What a place!"

At that Jim, Rob's brother walked back into the shop. "What's going on, Rob?" he asked.

"These cheeky sods just accused me of starting the fire," he replied.

"Typical! If your face don't fit you've had it. Our trouble, Rob, is that we ain't with the union; we ain't one of the boys, else we would be praised and given a medal for noticing the fire. Instead, they support the gaffers attacking us. We have to work to the clock; we can't get our day in and read the paper for an hour – only those in the union can get away with that. We have to fend for ourselves," stated Jim; "union don't look after us."

At that, Dago and I walked back to the sanding area, in fits of laughter. As we approached, we were immediately approached by Arthur. "What started the fire? Rob smoking?"

"Course it was," Dago replied; "the source of the fire was directly below where he smokes his fags. Bloody nutter."

"Well, you can't be really sure of that," I said; "anything might have started it. The fact is that those ducts should have been inspected and cleaned out regularly, and they never were. Whether a stub-end caused it or not is irrelevant; the ducts should never be in the state they were. Management have now got to get them cleaned out, or find themselves being prosecuted under the H and S

A W A, 1974," I went on to say.

"You've got an answer for everything," Arthur said, angrily. "Rob would be sacked anywhere else, and you know it. It is immediate dismissal for smoking in the woodshop. Christ almighty, Mac, he's putting our lives at risk."

Dago joined in: "I agree with Arthur; Rob and his brother aren't concerned one little bit. They actually accused me and Mac of being in a special little clique, who had it easy and could get away with anything. And, what's more, that we were accusing them of starting the fire because they weren't part of the clique."

"I hope you gave it them in the neck," Arthur replied.

"Well, to be honest we couldn't stop laughing, so we just walked away," answered Dago.

"As a union bloke, Mac, you'll stand for coal cracking on your head if you will stand for that," said Arthur.

"Arthur, you were right when you said we needed a rest room. What do you expect Rob or anyone else to do? Which would you prefer: spending your break outside, by the toilets, or in the shop? All of us should have a separate eating place," I said, meaningfully.

"Okay, but that doesn't excuse you for being too soft. Rob smokes in the shop, starts a fire and then, by using Health and

Safety nonsense, you get him off the hook. And, what's more, he attacks you for doing it. If he thinks he's got it hard on the bandsaw, tell him I'll swap with him, and he can try to earn his money on the bench," replied Arthur.

"Don't know if I agree with that, Arthur," said Dago; "the field far away always seems to be the greenest from a distance. Anyhow, Rob ain't that bad a bloke."

"Go on, clear off the both of you; I've got work to do, even if you two haven't. I have to earn every penny; nobody gives me anything for nothing – unlike some," Arthur replied, teasingly. Both Dago and I walked away with large grins on our faces.

No machining was being carried out for the rest of the day, as management had sent a team of labourers in to clean the underground ducting out; the only people who were able to work were those on the bench: i.e. Arthur.

It soon got around, what Arthur had said about Rob. This led Rob to purposefully walk by the benches, on his way for a smoke. As Rob walked by the bench, his brother Jim would put his head round the corner of the wall, by the spindle machine area, and look at Arthur. When Arthur noticed him, he would point and shout. "Look at that idle sod, off for a smoke." What annoyed Arthur was the fact that all of those laid off for the afternoon were being paid their average hourly rate; they hadn't been allowed to go home, so they had to hang around, waiting to start up again when the cleaning was finished. Arthur never replied to the goading by Rob and his brother at first, but by mid-afternoon Rob was passing Arthur's bench every fifteen minutes, to the annoyance of Arthur. By now, Rob was making remarks to him, on his way out. Fearing there might be trouble between Arthur and Rob, Dago came and fetched me from the stewards' office. I came back and hovered around the sanders, waiting to see if Rob would taunt Arthur anymore. He did: I looked around and could see Jim with his head popped round the corner, staring at Arthur. Then, Rob walked over to the benches on his way out, with his fags in his hand. As he approached the benches, he shouted: "Got time for a smoke, Arthur? I've got all the time in the world. You want to get yourself a job like mine, where you get smoke time. What's wrong? Can't you drag yourself away?" At this, Jim was howling with laughter, and the sanders were laughing, too. When Kelly walked into the shop, to go to his office, Rob told him: "Just going for a smoke." Kelly looked somewhat bemused and didn't reply.

Now red in the face, Arthur slammed down his spokeshave, took the wood he was working on out of his vice and slammed it on the bench. Then, he took out his chair and sat on it, declaring:

"I'm not doing another stroke. Sod it! The trouble with this place is that if your face fits you're made; if it doesn't you end up like me, working your bollocks off while everyone around is idling and taking the piss."

I immediately had a word with Rob and Jim, who were in fits of laughter at Arthur's response. They agreed to pack it in. I then had a word with Arthur: "Look, Arthur, the management won't pay you for doing nothing, no matter what I say or do."

"Couldn't care less. If those bastards ain't working then neither am I, and it's your fault for stopping the management from managing: they should have been able to discipline Rob and you stopped them," replied Arthur.

"Let's wait and see who's right or wrong, shall we? The fire officer is coming in anytime now; let's see what he has to say, shall we?"

"I'm not moving, anyway," Arthur replied.

Late that afternoon, a fire officer turned up, with a couple of lower-ranking officers, to carry out an inspection. Of course, by this time the ducts were cleared of all dust and any evidence of fire. In their verbal report, the fire officers made it clear that dust should be removed regularly. They also suggested that the smouldering could have been caused by a drop of water in the dust.

Apparently, in an enclosed area this can cause combustion; they went on to give some scientific explanation. Whatever, that report suited me fine. Most of the lads had had a rest day and probably stopped any future fires. Arthur continued to do his work but, as Dago pointed out to me: "He'd got his day in and wanted an excuse to stop work."

Discussion about the fire continued for a week or so. It had got around the factory that the union had threatened the management with strike action if they were to discipline Rob, because he was in with the union. I managed to get the report from the fire officers typed and placed on all noticeboards throughout the factory – this helped to put an end to such discussions.

14

Siege of Kelly's Office

We had all noticed that Sticky Dicky was getting even thicker with Kelly. Kelly had by now lost his bite, and had become the centre of ridicule by the woodshop. He had ended up virtually no more than a progress chaser – that, along with an affinity for walking, suited him to a tee. Although he was a foreman, his authority had somewhat diminished over the years, with opposition from the union. He had become a clear embarrassment to senior management. But, he was still management, and still took a delight in worrying people. It was strongly felt that it was Sticky Dicky who had informed Kelly about Rob, and it was Kelly going about his walks that spread the malicious rumours.

The only way of achieving the rest room was by seeking information from Sticky Dicky, and the only way the woodshop was ever going to achieve the rest room was by getting Kelly's office. But the gaffers weren't just gonna give us one; we would have to take it. "Kelly's Siege" would have to be a planned takeover.

I had deliberately shown little interest in Kelly moving to the shop next door; I didn't want the gaffers to know I was interested, even though I had been told in passing that Kelly was moving and his office would become a storeroom. I deliberately returned to the woodshop from the stewards' office five minutes early for my break, knowing that Sticky Dicky would be the first at the tea urn, so I could easily bump into him.

"Alright, Dick? Won't be long before Kelly's office has gone, then?" I said.

"Next Monday they're moving him," he answered.

"Who? Contractors?"

"No, they're emptying the stores room in the assembly shop and moving the stuff into the warehouse, then Kelly moves into what was the stores room," he answered.

"No contractors?" I asked.

"No, just our maintenance crew," he replied.

"Just the two of them?" I asked.

"Yes, it won't take two minutes to remove his phone and take what he needs from his office," replied Sticky Dicky.

"But I thought it was to be a storeroom?"

"Nah, the space will be used to accommodate trucks and

baskets of work waiting for the bench hands – save them being put all over the place," he replied.

"So, the maintenance crew – consisting of two – will be moving in and dismantling as soon as Kelly moves out on Monday?" I asked.

"You bet; that office will be gone in less than an hour," Sticky Dicky replied.

I couldn't believe my luck. When Arthur found out the whole world would be able to see what work he had done and was still waiting for him, he would be furious. For, Arthur had always given the appearance of never having much work and being reliant on others – this would disclose that as a myth, with at least a whole week's work waiting for him. This would surely stir Arthur into action.

The following Monday, I called a shop meeting, informing them that if they wanted a rest room, action would have to be taken. That action would consist of seizing Kelly's office as soon as it was vacated. If not, it would be used to store baskets, consisting of work waiting for the bench.

Arthur was the first to speak: "I don't smoke, but for those that do, there should be a place for them. Even if you don't smoke, there should be a room away from the dust and machines where you can go."

"I reckon that's right," said Bren.

"Why shouldn't we have the office? All the bleeding gaffers do," said Derek, from the sanders.

"I've always believed in rest rooms for those who work," said Rob. At that, Arthur's face turned evil, while Rob just laughed.

Sid, who chain-smoked, said: "Don't bother me either way; I shall continue to go outside for a fag, anyhow."

"Hold on a minute," said Micko, "this spray booth is bloody awful; we need a rest room, kiddo. It's alright for you lot: you ain't got a mask on all day. Right on, we need a rest room, kiddo."

"I'm like Sid: I'll support you, but I will be carrying on as normal, going outside," stated Sticky Dicky, even though we all knew that at break times he hid behind a board and smoked in the shop.

So, I put it to the vote and it was unanimous. "Right, as soon as Kelly has taken his things from the office, we occupy it until the gaffers agree it becomes our rest room. Everyone agree?"

We had held the meeting in the spray shop, where no one could actually see us. We then returned to the woodshop, and Kelly's office was already empty. Obviously, calling the meeting when I did, in the spray shop, had stopped Sticky Dicky being able to warn Kelly. "Right, lads," I said, "occupy the office until management agree." This was duly done. Out came the cards, teapots and papers; everybody was enjoying themselves, though Sticky Dicky was uneasy, and kept leaving the office, with any excuse he could.

Within half an hour, I left the office to call a meeting of all the shop stewards. I informed the stewards what was going on in regard to the siege, and each steward gave their support. Each had informed their foreman that they were off for a meeting, and it was agreed that, on their return, each steward would not let on what was discussed. But Malek (steward), once he had been put under pressure by his foreman, would in confidence leak that if the management did not give way by the end of the day, the stewards would recommend to their members to join the siege and, in doing so, would involve the media. The publicity, we hoped, would be bad for the company.

I returned to the siege, to find the lads were enjoying themselves, delighted at what I had to report. With the extractor off it had the feeling of Christmas about it.

Two hours into the siege came the two maintenance crew, to dismantle the office. They were met with Arthur, who said to them: "There's a dispute on. Come back when it is settled."

"Look, we have got a job to do and we're going to do it. We aren't in dispute," said the electrician.

"That's right: we aren't involved and we've got a job to do," said the other maintenance bloke, meaningfully.

"Now, look here, lads. Respect our dispute; the entrance to the office is a picket line," I replied.

"Okay, we'll dismantle the office from outside the picket line," said the electrician.

At this point everybody had clambered around the office door, looking at the maintenance blokes. "Dismantle this office and I'll dismantle you, piece by piece!" shouted Bren.

The electrician looked me straight in the eye. "You're not going to allow one of your members to threaten us like that, are you?"

"Well, if you clear off you won't be a threat to us and my members won't be a threat to you. Now, just bloody clear off," I replied.

They just stood there as if they were preparing for a stand-off. I moved slowly through the office door to face the two straight on; slowly, everyone else moved from the office and joined me. We moved forward one pace, and they stayed exactly where they were, just two paces away. So, I moved another pace toward them, and within two seconds everyone had joined me. Then the maintenance crew fled – obviously to their own rest room; even though there were only two of them, they had their own rest room with tea-making facilities, a radio and a T.V. How they managed to accumulate so much and do so much work to make their rest room so comfy I'll never know; as far as I can remember they only ever had two pairs of hands between them.

By twelve o'clock Mr. Wales had sent for me. "What is this ridiculous situation regarding you and your members occupying Mr. Kelly's old office?"

Realizing now that he was expecting the whole of the factory to get involved, I knew I could be onto a winner. "Simply, if anyone is to have the office it should be us. If ever anybody deserved a rest from the dust and noise it's us," I replied.

"Look here, why didn't you just mention this some time ago? We might have been able to work something out."

"Because you were going to turn the area into a store area for baskets of work; you never gave us a second thought. You know very well we haven't got a rest room – it's no secret; the whole world and his wife know we haven't got one," I replied.

"That's no excuse for this. If you had just approached us in the normal way, we could have come to an arrangement," he stated, firmly.

"Well, hopefully now you will," I answered.

"Obviously I won't be paying you for the dispute. But I will be back within the hour, and I would expect you all to return to work while I consider your request," Wales said.

"And, of course, we would expect you not to try dismantling the office while considering," I replied.

"Of course," replied Wales.

So, we all went back to work. One and a half hours later Wales ask to see me. "I can see no reason why Kelly's old office cannot be turned into a rest room. Obviously, I expect it not to be abused, and that it put an end to anyone thinking of smoking in the woodshop," he stated.

"Of course, and thank you very much," I replied, gleefully. I then informed the woodshop, with some delight, that we had achieved something constructive.

Sticky Dicky had been somewhat surprised at our achievement, and it wasn't until later that he spread the rumour that the woodshop had saved the company a considerable amount in insurance fees, because having a separate smoking room decreased the risk of fire. That possibility could have some truth in it, but what it really did was bring all the members of the shop together each break time, where matters of importance and general concern were discussed, and grievances aired. Most importantly, though, solidarity was underlined. The company may have saved a few pounds on insurance costs, but the workers had saved tremendously when it came to the social cost.

15

Peace Time

It was 1982. We'd had a few small disputes; people had come and gone. My deputy Chitty had left and been replaced by Johnny, a slim Irishman in his mid-thirties. He mirrored himself on Clint Eastwood, but he was a real good guy and trade unionist; if you got to the wire, he would still be there, by your side.

Times had changed with Thatcher in charge. Leading stewards in the car plants had been sacked. However, we still had reasonable pay and conditions, although we'd had a few minor disputes since the Setters' Strike. At this time we were very active, joining marches and campaigns to protect our union's hard-fought gains.

Health and Safety had always been one of our priorities, and we had made great headway and won a couple of awards for our endeavours, continually improving the health and safety of members, and conditions in general. Meetings were held monthly with management, which enabled us to nip problems in the bud before they escalated into major disputes – the Works Committee felt, as I did, that the meetings were very productive and benefitted us all.

4. Johnny, my deputy.

At one meeting, Wales had shared his concern with us regarding the Countryside Bill that was going through Parliament, and how it could affect us detrimentally. I contacted the local M.P. Roy Hattersley, who agreed to meet Wales and myself in Parliament the next day, to discuss the bill and how it could be amended, in a way not to be detrimental to us.

Off we both went the next day, on the train to London. This was a bit awkward for me, as I had nothing in common with Wales, so the hours we spent together that day were purgatory – although he did introduce me to his favourite drink: a gin and tonic; the tonic had to be Indian. We arrived at Parliament and were taken to where Roy Hattersley would be. As we walked toward his office, he came out with his personal secretary to meet us. He walked straight up to us and asked: "Which one of you is Peter McDonald?"

"I am," I replied, a little nervously. He then shook my hand and welcomed us into his office, where we discussed the bill and possible amendments. I really appreciated the way he had welcomed us, and going straight to me was golden; poor old Wales was out of it. Amendments did go through, which meant the bill was no longer a threat to the company's future.

The meeting was not always about improving terms and conditions; we would often make it clear to management our concerns regarding poor work. Quite often our members would be threatened with disciplinary action because of poor quality, even though previously they had already complained to the foreman regarding faulty component parts, being told to carry on assembling the parts to complete the product. Then, when the inspector refused to pass the work, the inspector would be overruled, the products would go for distribution and, of course, the member got the blame. With the amount of faulty goods leaving the company we were now starting to get a bad name. This led us to suggest at one of the meetings that a rectification book be produced and put into practice.

It comprised a number of pages made up of plain paper and carbon paper, so that, whatever was written, a copy was made. As soon as a worker realized parts were faulty, he/she would stop work and inform the foreman; the foreman would then have to sign the first page of the book, stating how many of these components would be allowed to go through, and sign it; a copy would then go to the superintendent, who would have to countersign; a copy would then go to Black, the manager; and finally to Wales. for his acknowledgement. So, we had things in reverse order: the operator would call the foremen to sign, then the foreman called in the superintendent to sign, then the superintendent called in the manager to sign, then finally the works director was called in to approve the actions of all those under him. As you can imagine, neither the foreman nor the superintendent were happy with this, as there would be evidence of them approving the assembly of faulty components. However, such a suggestion would be hard for Wales to object to, so it was agreed and put into practice. Within a short time, the machines producing poor quality parts were rectified, and the quality of goods improved dramatically. Of course, it also showed up setters and tool setters for not rectifying the machines in the first place, and joining management in blaming the operators and assemblers.

Both Johnny and I believed we were doing alright with management, and were working constructively together. Trade was not fantastic, but we had shown them we were concerned and constructive in our talks. We felt we were all working together in the interests of the company. Although trade wasn't that great, compared to other businesses we were doing well, and things looked settled for the future.

But I was in a fool's paradise; the disputes of all disputes was just around the corner.

16

Outbreak of War

The first sign of a major dispute came as Johnny and I were on our way to our normal monthly meeting with management. The office we held our meetings in was on the top floor, where all the main offices were located. As we walked along the corridor to the office we were to meet in, we would always have a peep in the rooms as we walked by.

I opened the door of one of the larger rooms and, to my horror and astonishment, components of all the rifles were displayed on a large table, with name tags on. A shiver went down my spine. I turned to Johnny, who represented the machine shop on the first floor; "You know what this is all about, don't you?"

"No, but I don't like it," he replied, shaking his head.

"All our components are on show. That can only mean one thing: for interested engineering firms to put in bids to make the parts," I said, angrily.

We decided not to bring this up at the meeting with

management, but soon as the meeting was finished we would call a meeting of all the shop stewards. The stewards' meeting was duly held, and I opened up by explaining what Johnny and myself had seen in the room. One of the components displayed was trigger guards. This was a most boring job to machine, and they were done in their thousands, usually when a machinist had run out of work; these were known as "filling-in jobs". I asked the stewards the last time any of their machinists had worked on trigger guards, and Abdul responded immediately: "Now you mention it, we haven't done any for well over a year. So, who's been doing them?"

This got the rest of the stewards thinking; at least ten components on display, which were seen as filling-in jobs, had not been worked on for well over a year. So, as Abdul said: "Who's been doing them?" I made the obvious assumption that they had been outsourced to undoubtedly non-union factories: done on the cheap in poor conditions. Furthermore, the company was obviously satisfied with work being outsourced, and what we witnessed was a means of inviting tenders.

"Our jobs are on the line," I stressed, most strongly.

"Christ, the bastards! We've got to do something. The bastards!" said Johnny, visually shaking in temper.

It was agreed that Johnny and myself would call a meeting with management, to get some assurances: firstly, that trigger guards and other components return in-house; secondly, that there are no plans to shut any of the machine shops. What I did not know was that plans to shut the woodshop were already at an advanced stage. We met management and demanded those assurances. Black and Wales were present at the meeting.

The response we received from Wales was exactly what we feared: "We have the right to manage and do business with whomever we wish to, and will not give you such assurances. It is our right to do whatever we feel is in the interests of the business. Good day."

Cocky, no-good bastard, I thought to myself.

We reported to a stewards' meeting immediately. Rumours were now flying around the factory, which we knew would happen, with so many meetings being held. I had the difficult task of being honest with the stewards, pointing out that the company is in the process of outsourcing our jobs and livelihoods. We were all aware that unemployment was now over a million, and jobs with our pay and conditions were like gold dust. Knowing the situation the country was in, especially with a trade union-hating government, we still decided to take on management with the threat of strike action.

A mass meeting was called and I put it to the members to try and remember the last time they had worked on trigger guards and similar components. The penny dropped, and they realized some of their work was already being done outside. I put it to them: "This is not about some infringement of an agreement; we are fighting the ultimate battle: the battle for our livelihoods and the food on our tables. They have started the process of outsourcing and all we have is the weapon of mass disruption of their plans."

The meeting unanimously agreed that we should enter into a dispute.

Memoirs of early working life

5. The Works Committee proudly marching through Birmingham with our own bespoke banner, on a glorious summer day. The banner was designed by Graham Stevenson (who went on to become a national officer for the T. & G. W. U.), and sewed and stitched together by my partner Christine. We still have the banner some forty years later, ready to use at a moment's notice.

17

Battle Lines Being Drawn

We reported immediately back to management. "Thank you and good day," responded Wales, in a cocky, snobbish fashion.

This time we didn't just walk out straight away; after the experience of the Setters Dispute, we would have a strategy. Our plan was to ask the packers who despatched the final goods to stop work, and the rest of us still working would club together and fund their wages. This had the advantage of the management forking out wages while their income stream dried up. Without the packers working, nothing could leave the warehouse. It worked well for two weeks, until the management laid off a number of employees who supplied the packers. It became impossible to fund the number of members now not in work.

So, the inevitable happened: we went on strike.

The next part of our plan would be a "work-in". We managed, from our union funds, to purchase a number of camp beds. We then set up a shift pattern for stewards, ensuring the factory was inhabited for twenty-four hours, seven days a week, making sure nothing got in and nothing got out. The warehouse was now overflowing with orders waiting to be despatched. At night, we would sleep in turns; some of us slept in the "Hut", others in the print room. Wherever we slept, the factory was another world at night; it was cold, eerie, and all we could hear while trying to get off to sleep were the rats, scratching and chewing around us.

6. Stewards in the "Hut" having a bit of a laugh, not knowing what was around the corner. Like most unionists at the time we smoked a lot; just look at the three packets of cigarettes on the table. All around the panelling of the "Hut" were cuttings of successful campaigns; you will note the call for a 35-hour week. Little did we know at the time that the "Hut" would be shortly used as a place to bed down for a number of weeks, and become our second home.

Our main concern of a night was that anyone could get easy access into the factory, and take whatever weapons they fancied – and our worry was that the I.R.A. just might try. This made us carry out patrols and set booby traps at each door which gave access to the factory. This consisted of gun barrels being placed on top of doors set ajar; if you tried to open the door, you would be seriously hurt. Of course, looking back, we should have realized that if anyone was going to try a break-in, the police would have been patrolling on the insistence of the company.

It would be days before most of us would see our families; we took the "work-in" seriously. After a number of weeks, we were scavenging scrap from the old motorbike buildings which were being demolished – this was the only way we could get our hands on any cash. At time, scavenging could be a bit upsetting; we were scavenging scrap from where the bombs old Tom told me about had hit, and we could see where the concrete had been filled in, therefore sealing off any chance of getting the bodies out. The managing director of the contracting company carrying out the demolition caught us scavenging, but he was good as gold, saying: "Leave my stuff alone and you can help yourself." A welcome relief.

Six weeks had passed, and most stewards, quite rightly, had to spend more time with their families, which left me and Johnny on our own quite often, patrolling at night. We were aware that if anyone tried their luck they could easily overpower us, get hold of weapons and ammunition and be off. It could be at least five days before we would see our families, but we stood solidly. Looking back, we put our families under extreme stress and anxiety, not knowing where the money was coming from, for the next meal on the table. Over six weeks had passed, and management were now sending letters out to our members stating that if they didn't return to work they would lose their jobs, putting their families under pressure to return them to work.

We therefore had little option but to call a mass meeting on Monday, eight weeks into the strike. Unfortunately, I had no knowledge that the foremen, along with their superintendents, were stopping members as they entered the road which led to the factory. The members were being threatened and intimidated by their superiors, and many had turned back and gone home. Had we known this was going on, we would have made sure stewards were positioned at the top of the road, warning off the gaffers and protecting our members' right to democratically participate in their future.

The meeting was held in the car park, at the rear of the company. I put it to the meeting that the dispute should continue. It was obvious to all of us there that many loyal supporters had not turned up, but I could not delay the vote being taken.

7. A bitterly cold day in Liverpool. But not as bitter as losing the fight for our livelihoods.

It was that close that the only way to be sure who was voting for what was to ask those supporting the continuation of the strike to walk over to the right of the car park, and those against to walk over to the left. The vote to continue was lost by four votes, which was very upsetting, when considering what we had put our families through. In addition, if our loyal supporters had not been intimidated and threatened, the dispute would have continued. Nearly two hundred turned out, yet over two hundred and fifty were involved in the dispute.

18

Battle Lost

We all returned to work with our tails between our legs. There was an atmosphere of foreboding and the writing was on the wall; we were to lose our jobs.

The second day back, Rob, working on the ripsaw, had his face split open by a piece of wood, which bounced back off the saw and struck him in the face. I immediately followed my accident procedures, taking photos of the scene, interviewing witnesses and telling them to tell management as little as possible – and, of course, Rob not to speak to the management at all. With training I had received through the union, we had yet to lose a case, and I certainly did not want to lose this one. However, no matter what, Rob would be scarred.

The third day back, I got called to a meeting with management, expecting to be informed of redundancies in the machine shops, because of the outsourcing of their work. I walked up the familiar steps to the conference room with Johnny, both forlorn and almost sulking. We entered the room and there were Wales, Wax and Black, like magistrates.

8. The Works Committee had just finished a march around Birmingham, with the sun shining on the righteous in brighter times.

"Good morning," Wales said, opening the meeting. "Just to inform you that we have set in motion plans to shut the woodshop and have the stocks imported, using the space for other purposes. Therefore, I am giving you notice, gentlemen. Good day."

As we walked down the stairs from the conference room, Jonny said: "What the bloody hell do we do now?"

"I'll inform the woodshop right now. No doubt they'll stop

work and all hell will break out," I responded, more in shock than anger.

We had in the past negotiated some good terms and conditions, such as a redundancy agreement which consisted of average earnings for your entitled notice period, up to twelve weeks, and an extra week's pay for every year worked. The first thing management did on our first day back was to put on the noticeboards that all negotiated agreements were now null and void, because of the financial state the company found themselves, as a result of the strike.

A meeting was held in the woodshop and all hell broke loose, as I predicted. Bren shouted: "Stuff the bastards! Stuff the place! Burn it to the ground, I reckon!"

Arthur joined in: "We've been shafted by those arse-licking bastards who voted to return. They ain't gonna support us; we're on our own."

Derek joined in, viciously: "Bugger the place. Let's get as much as we can and get out of the place."

No vote was taken to stop work; work was just never going to happen now. Micko from the spray shop said, in a rational voice: "Derek's right. Let's get as much as we can and bugger off."

Nobody from anywhere else was anywhere near the

woodshop; it was like people knew better than to enter. The mood in the woodshop was volatile and at flashpoint; anyone who had voted to return, brave enough to walk through the shop, would have been lynched.

The lads in the woodshop were united in one thing: they were going to get the redundancy agreement negotiated by the union, no matter what. I suggested that we all meet Wales together, and we don't leave the conference room without the right money. I rang Wales and asked to see him; he immediately agreed. Then, all ten of us walked up the stairs into the conference room. There were Wales, Wax and Black, already waiting for us. I opened up coolly and rationally: "We want to be paid our notice in lieu and the negotiated redundancy agreement in full, and we will pack up tonight." Nobody else from the woodshop spoke. There was no need to: we spoke in one voice.

Wales replied: "Thank you for that, but as you are fully aware, we no longer have the money for such agreements, after weeks of lost production. We have little money. You will receive your legal entitlement, gentlemen."

I looked him straight in his gin and tonic eyes and replied: "I am not interested in you having little money. You caused the dispute and we have no money because of you. Now, just pay up and honour an agreement, for once in your life."

"Let me tell you, you have no right to anything. I have to think of the future of the company, and those still working here – that's who I have a responsibility to. That's it, gentlemen," he replied, cockily.

There was an eerie quiet, as though a bomb was about to go off. I stood up, looked down at Wales and said, in an aggressive and determined voice: "You will pay us now, in lieu of notice and based on the agreed redundancy terms – right now!" I then looked at Bren and said: "Guard that door; nobody leaves this room until we get what we are entitled to." Then, I turned to Wales and said: "Now, pay up or else."

His face turned white and ashen. The atmosphere was tense. Wales was faced with a group of people who had nothing to lose: we had no money, no jobs and a bleak future ahead of us. The three of them were now facing the consequences of their actions, and knew now that it was either pay up or... I wasn't quite sure myself... be locked in with a group of people who were far from happy, perhaps.

As I stood looking down at Wales, he coughed and said: "Gentlemen, I will honour my agreement, but not now."

I just stared at him and said, forcefully: "Pay now; get your cheque book out. Bren, stay at that door; no one leaves this room."

Wales turned to Wax, the financial director, and they both froze for a moment. Then, from Wax's inside pocket came a cheque book, and from Wales's inside pocket a sheet of paper. "Gentlemen, I will give you all a cheque, but it can't be cashed for five days." We looked at each other and, without hesitation, agreed on those terms.

We left the room with smiles on our faces; we'd got a good settlement. On the way down those familiar steps from the conference room, Bren said, proudly: "They shit themselves, didn't they, you reckon?"

Arthur, now in his late fifties, remarked: "This suits me; I ain't complaining."

Derek, now in his usual calm manner, said: "Well we couldn't have got any more. With this sort of money, I'll have a few days off before looking for work."

We all returned to the woodshop, heads held high and feeling rather pleased with ourselves. Then we all cleared up, gathered what tools we had and emptied our lockers. On top of the redundancy money we had as pieceworkers, we also had what was known as "work at the back of the book": this was simply work which had been done but never booked in (claimed for). It was generally for a rainy day or holiday week, known as "pudding week". Most of us had about three weeks' worth of work not booked. Of course, we now booked it in, so we had an additional three weeks' pay coming to us.

While cleaning out my locker, I was approached by the superintendent, who demanded the noise counter and the pollution gauge I had in my possession. He had obviously really approached me to have some fun, now that I was finished. "This is the property of the elected convenor, as these appliances are concerned with Health and Safety," I stated.

He just looked at me and said: "Just hand them over."

"Never," I replied. "They will be handed over to Johnny, who is now the elected convenor."

He left and returned with Johnny, who I gave the appliances to – my last action as the convenor, proud that I had never given in to a gaffer to the end.

There was no booze-up; we all just went home with the cheques in our pockets.

Peter McDonald

9. *It may be over, but only for now.*

19

Directed Into the World of Education

I never had much contact with those who gave so much, united, to improve our working lives. Derek moved to Blackpool, where his wife came from, and was doing well. I did receive an unexpected invite to Arthur's seventieth birthday from his son. All the others just disappeared and went their different ways.

I kept up going to branch meetings on a Friday night, to keep in touch. Like most active stewards at the time, being blacklisted made it extremely hard to find employment.

I had a chance encounter with a fellow steward from years previously, at a Labour Party Meeting in Redditch. His name was Joe. Originally from Glasgow, he smoked a pipe, and his accent reminded me of my granddad, who was also from Glasgow. We had been active together around 1968, demonstrating outside the offices of B S A – known as the Golden Mile – in an effort to save the motorcycle industry. The demonstration had turned into a bit of a riot, so it was unlikely we would ever forget it. He asked how

I was doing. I made the point clear that I was out of work. "Get yourself educated and move into another area," he advised me. "You are not going to get a job in a factory again." He was a good ten years older than me, and I really warmed to him.

It was the summer of 1982, and Joe advised me to try and get into Fircroft College for Mature Students, in Selly Oak. Realizing it was late summer and the new academic year was to start shortly, I didn't believe I would have a chance of getting enrolled. However, I passed the initial test and managed to get in. The one thing I was short of was books, and they weren't cheap. But the union was good as gold, and gave me enough money to buy the books required. So, off I went as a mature student.

The help I received at the college was tremendous, and not in any patronizing manner. I received one-to-one tutorials and, because of my dedication, I managed to get extra. I would act as though I was still working in a factory, working to a set time and being disciplined; I would arrive early in the morning and leave at five in the evening, which was late for a student. This really did benefit me; lecturers noticed this and therefore gave me extra tutorials and support. I mainly studied economics, along with politics and some sociology.

The hard work and discipline paid off, when I managed to gain a place at Wolverhampton Polytechnic on a Social Science degree course. Once again, I received help and support to get me through. I even transferred from Social Science for a year, to be qualified in Industrial Law. I was determined that I would educate myself to fight Thatcher. For the majority of time I was a student, I qualified for a mature student grant – something I have Harold Wilson to thank for.

By 1986, I had achieved a 2.2 honours in Social Science, and was dead chuffed. But, I could not have done it without the support of my wife Christine and my daughters Karen and Julie; they all went without for some years. And not forgetting the union, who supported me at every stage – and, of course, Joe, for pointing me in the right direction.

20

The Struggle Continues

While a student at Wolverhampton I became involved in the Students' Union and the Labour Club, in particular. I was engaged in fighting Militant Tendency who, in my opinion, were wrecking the Labour Party.

The girlfriend of one of the leaders of the Militants was a student; he had treated her badly, for whatever reason, and she had left him. However, when she left him she took a load of his stuff with her, but what she kept was dynamite, such as collecting tins "for the miners", but when the stickers were removed it said, clear as day, "Militant Tendency". There was also a considerable amount of correspondence, relating to plans to wreck Labour Party meetings and take over key positions within the party. I sent all the stuff to the secretary of the Telford Labour Party, who sent the stuff to H.Q. Neil Kinnock had enough evidence to challenge Militant Tendency, which helped bring them down.

After four years of studying, it was time to call it a day in education and look for employment. It was not easy, even with a decent degree, to get an interview, let alone a job. However, I was fortunate enough in the recent past to have met Derek Robinson ("Red Robbo") regarding an unfair dismissal case we were both helping out with. Unlike the way he was portrayed by the media, he was a very kind and considerate person. He had heard I was looking for work and pointed me toward Bilston College, where he had been doing some work for the T.U.C.

By now I had got cheesed off spending a great deal of time putting letters and my C.V. together, when applying for jobs. However, as Derek had contacted me, I gave it a go. I put all my details on one page of a notebook and sent it off to the contact Derek had given me. Was I surprised when I had a reply, inviting me for an interview?! I was fortunate enough to be accepted for part-time work, which I grabbed with two hands. It eventually led to a full-time position.

It was sometime later that I found out why I got the interview, despite simply applying on a piece of notepaper. Apparently, the head of the department showed my application to his wife, saying: "Just look at the nerve of this guy, applying on a shoddy piece of notepaper." His wife had commented: "Who the hell is he?" They looked at the name and address, then the head of department said:

"Hold on, that name rings a bell." He checked it out, then said to his wife: "This is from the guy who sent me all that stuff on Militant Tendency. The least I can do is give him an interview."

That led to me into teaching for twenty years, and I enjoyed all of it – especially being able to carry out work for the T.U.C., educating shop stewards the best I could. I had ensured that I got my own back on Thatcher, who weakened the trade unions with her draconian legislation, by preparing people for the struggle ahead, for equality and justice.

In 1985, I became an elected councillor on Hereford and Worcestershire County Council, and in 1990 a Bromsgrove district councillor.

Without unions we would all be trodden on and fed to the wolves. United we stand, divided we fall!

Acknowledgments

The publisher would like to thank Russell Spencer, Matt Vidler, Laura-Jayne Humphrey, Lianne Bailey-Woodward, Leonard West, Janelle Hope and Susan Woodard for their hard work and efforts in bringing this book to publication.

About the Publisher

L.R. Price Publications is dedicated to publishing books by unknown authors.

We use a mixture of both traditional and modern publishing options, to bring our authors' words to the wider world.

We print, publish, distribute and market books in a variety of formats including paper and hardback, electronic books, digital audiobooks and online.

If you are an author interested in getting your book published, or a book retailer interested in selling our books, please contact us.
www.lrpricepublications.com

L.R. Price Publications Ltd,
27 Old Gloucester Street,
London, WC1N 3AX.
020 3051 9572

publishing@lrprice.com

Memoirs of early working life

Printed in Great Britain
by Amazon